BEARING
FRUIT

BEARING FRUIT

MINISTRY WITH REAL RESULTS

LOVETT H. WEEMS JR.
TOM BERLIN

Abingdon Press
Nashville

BEARING FRUIT
MINISTRY WITH REAL RESULTS

Copyright © 2011 by Abingdon Press

Library of Congress Cataloging-in-Publication Data

Berlin, Tom.
    Bearing fruit : ministry with real results / Tom Berlin and Lovett H. Weems Jr.
        p. cm.
    ISBN 978-1-4267-1590-7 (book—pbk./trade pbk., adhesive—perfect binding : alk. paper)
    1. Discipling (Christianity)   2. Spiritual formation.   3. Church work.   4. Evangelistic work.
I. Weems, Lovett H. (Lovett Hayes)   II. Title.
    BV4520.B393 2011
    253'.7--dc22

                                                                                    2011004786

11 12 13 14 15 16 17 18 19 20—10 9 8 7 6 5 4 3 2 1

MANUFACTURED IN THE UNITED STATES OF AMERICA

To
my wife, Karen,
and our daughters Rebekah, Kathryn, Hannah, and Sarah,
I know of few vocations that involve a family more than being
a pastor. Your encouragement, insights, and honesty have been
a means of grace. You have my love and gratitude.
T. B.

To
my wife, Emily,
with much love and appreciation,
and to our children and grandchildren,
the blessing of our lives
L. H. W.

CONTENTS

Introduction

A Call from the Church for Fruitful Leadership

A Tale of Two Churches

Driving down the back road in a rural community, Tom could see a familiar structure up ahead. The peaked roof, row of windows, and prominent front door with a small bell tower above made it easy for him to guess that he was coming up on a church building.

> I had just passed one a few miles back. That church was also easy to identify. It was a wooden structure with a fresh coat of white paint, flowers lining the sidewalk, and a small sign outside that provided the church name and worship times. The appearance of the church and grounds made it clear that many people cared a great deal about their church and its ministry.
>
> As I got closer to the second church, I could see that it had been a long time since anyone had cared for it. The paint had worn off the building's exterior. The glass was missing from the window panes. The front steps had rotted, and some were missing. Despite its poor condition, the building was full. In fact, the small sanctuary was absolutely packed. I was so amazed by this sight that I stopped the car to examine it more closely. Looking in the windows, I could imagine the scripture being read, a chorus of voices joined in a hymn of praise, and children meeting in the back rooms for Sunday school. All I could see now, however, were bales of hay. A local farmer had converted the now dead church facility into a hay barn.

This book is about fruitful leadership. We believe that churches are called to be fruitful for God. The range of fruitfulness among churches has little to do with location or economics. Two churches just a few miles apart can have very different stories, outcomes, and impact on their community. We believe that one of the most important sources of fruitful ministry is the fruitful leadership of laypersons and pastors in the church. Before those leaders can be effective, they must believe the church is created by God to be fruitful. They must be convinced that when the church is fruitful, it will have ministry that matters to its community. They must also be convinced that when a church lacks fruitfulness, the end is closer than we may think.

It will not be fresh news to the reader of this book that the ministry of the church has long been judged to be in a period of decline in areas of effectiveness and impact. Most denominations and congregations maintain the tradition of year-end reporting that counts much of their ministry, including worship attendance; membership; expenditures; programs for children, youth, and adults; and special services throughout the year. For some denominations this list is quite extensive, and rarely is the compilation of such reports for a geographical region found to be a source of encouragement or celebration.

If the critique of the decline of the church's ministry were simply leveled by the society in which it finds itself, it would not be hard to take. We have grown accustomed, in every generation of history, to the criticisms of those who did not understand the intentions or passions of the Christian faith. We understand that the church, when most vital and most faithful, leaves its culture of residence scratching its head and wondering why the particular teachings and ways of Christ matter so dearly to us when they seem so out of place in the world.

The concern that leaders in the church properly carry is that many of those who judge its ministry and mission negatively are persons who are most familiar with its biblical mandates and theological heritage. They are pastors and highly committed laypersons who, as they grow older, carry a deep and imperative fear: that the ministry of the church will be fruitless in their generation. There are very few things worse for Christians than to know the transforming power of Christ in their own lives but fail to see it broadly at work in the world.

OBJECTIONS TO FRUITFULNESS

While many share a longing for fruitful ministry, much of the problem is within the leadership of the church itself. Listening carefully to discussion of clergy and laypersons within the church reveals vocabulary that contributes to the problem:

- "I am not called to be effective; I am called to be faithful." Generations of clergy have grown up with this saying, and it is often a response to declining numbers on the year-end reports. Obviously, there is deep truth in the statement. Of course, all Christian ministry is called to faithfulness. Not all of our impact can be recorded in statistical tables, and some ministry settings will seldom reward those who seek ever-increasing numbers. The problem with the statement, however, is that it promotes the idea that pastors and lay leaders have no responsibility for fruitfulness. This comment leads us to believe that fruitful ministry is somehow not faithful, and faithful ministry is not typically fruitful. And we fear some clergy use it to avoid an essential accountability beyond faithfulness.

- "I am called to a 'ministry of presence.'" This term suggests that leaders in congregations are not called to expend energy and time in helping a congregation discover a vision or create strategies to accomplish goals. Pastors transfer this term, properly taught in the context of pastoral care, to church leadership. This is a dangerous construct in the minds of pastors. It has the power to turn leaders into chaplains whose goal is simply to be with people rather than equip and encourage their growth or the use of their spiritual gifts for fruitful ministry.

- "You have to understand where we are in our life cycle as a congregation." It is difficult to lead a church with a 150-year history. It takes binoculars to look all the way back from your point of entry to the zeal that led the founders to establish that congregation. The sacrifice and focus that necessarily accompany planting a church may be a distant memory, if recalled at all. Although understanding the life cycle of the congregation is very helpful in assessing its strengths and weaknesses, it must not be used to squelch the theology of hope found in Christ's words, "Behold, I make all things new" (Revelation 21:5 KJV). It must not become an excuse for avoiding the call to fruitful ministry.

WHAT IS FRUITFUL LEADERSHIP?

"What is your ideal picture of the excellent pastoral leader of the future?"

An ecumenical gathering of church and seminary leaders reflected on this question. The first person to respond described the ideal pastoral leader as deeply grounded in the faith tradition, strongly connected to God, steeped in ongoing prayer, and faithful in taking weekly sabbath time. This picture of pastoral excellence resonated with many in the group.

Something, however, is glaringly missing from this picture. Thousands of congregations are in serious trouble. Children are not being taught the faith. Disciples are not being made. Lives are not being transformed. The poor are not being blessed. Communities are not being redeemed. These congregations know something is terribly wrong. And in most cases, the problems have little to do with the pastor's prayer life or whether the pastor takes weekly sabbath time. In fact, in many of these churches members deeply respect their pastors as sincerely spiritual people of utmost personal faith and integrity. But they need more from their pastoral leaders.

SO WHAT IS WRONG?

At the General Conference of The United Methodist Church in 1992, Bishop Dale White was delivering the Episcopal Address. This address is something like a State of the Union message for the denomination given by a bishop selected by the Council of Bishops. Just as with presidential State of the Union addresses, there are predictable times for applause and always those awkward moments when it is clear that the speaker anticipates applause and there is none. Equally surprising can be those times when spontaneous applause erupts at places where it was not anticipated or even desired.

Such was the case for Bishop White in 1992. The address was interrupted many times with applause, most coming at very predictable points. But there was that awkward moment when unanticipated applause came after these words: "We will assist ineffective clergy to seek another vocation...." Such moments tell us more than any survey can about what is troubling the church.

The church knows it needs more from its pastors. Some call for effectiveness or excellence. Others say we must have stronger leadership. The response to Bishop White's words reminds us that this is not a new issue, but it seems to have an intensity about it today that is different from some times in the past. Virtually every denominational judicatory has the subject of clergy effectiveness on its agenda. Most have developed leadership standards for clergy in recent years, pointing to the widespread concern that something is not right.

Pastoral leaders do not and should not think in terms of performance, but we must remember admonitions for effective leadership. As Paul put it: "If you are a leader, exert yourself to lead" (Romans 12:8b NEB).

A PLACE FOR CONTRIBUTION

Research conducted by the Lewis Center for Church Leadership of Wesley Theological Seminary[1] leads us to believe that clergy are doing very well in important aspects of leadership, but that there is a crucial missing piece represented by the concept of fruitful leadership.

The Lewis Center analyzed descriptions of clergy leadership expectations developed separately by numerous denominational judicatories with the goal of identifying the most common recurring features. Three primary categories seem to capture virtually all the specific descriptors of effectiveness:

1. "Character" or who the leader is;
2. "Competence" or what the leader knows and does; and
3. "Contribution" or what the leader accomplishes.

The first two categories are usually associated with faithful ministry. Character captures those characteristics of the leader as a person. These include matters of spiritual authenticity, integrity, and wholeness. Competence captures those characteristics of the leader as a religious professional. These include matters of biblical and theological knowledge; lifelong learning; ministry skills in preaching and other pastoral areas; relational skills; the ability to empower the leadership of others; judgment; and accountability.

The third category, Contribution, may hold the most potential for revitalized pastoral leadership. Contribution captures those characteristics of the leader as steward of the church's mission. These include working with a congregation to discern God's vision for them and guiding the implementation of the vision so that the congregation bears fruit—experiencing God's presence, transforming lives, growing disciples, and serving others.

Not surprisingly, this third component is the least developed in the judicatory descriptions studied by the Lewis Center. Serving institutions, such as churches and schools, tend to focus on "who we are," "what we do," and "how we do it." Very little attention is given to "what we accomplish."

WHAT EVALUATION IS MISSING?

To address "what we accomplish," we will need to examine the way we do evaluation in our churches. Many congregations now give attention to evaluating their projects and areas of ministry. But most of these evaluations may be missing a crucial element. They tend to ask participants how they experienced an event or how well a program was planned. Common topics reviewed in such evaluations include the preparations, materials, setup, individual elements of the program, and the rating or informal feedback from each participant. This is often called evaluating the *process*.

Such process evaluation gives helpful feedback for planning future events, but it does not answer the most important question, which is whether the effort achieved the *outcomes* that the project set out to accomplish. It may be that every aspect of the offering went superbly and that those attending learned a great deal and were inspired. But it still may not have achieved the desired outcomes.[2]

Some may question a focus on evaluating outcomes in the church because, they say, the church deals in intangibles that do not lend themselves to measurement. It is true that, although some goals of the church are easily quantifiable for measurement purposes, other goals are not so easily quantified. That does not mean, however, that they cannot be measured or assessed. Leaders can still determine whether there is improvement in achieving the outcomes sought. They can discern whether the mission of the church is helping shape its life and work.

The challenge is not so much that intangibles cannot be measured but that we often have not taken the time to clarify exactly what we mean by such intangibles. We may say that we want people to "experience God" or "grow in their walk with Christ" without working to clarify the meaning of those phrases. Asking, "What do you mean by that?" can help. Often the answer is that we have not thought much about what we mean; therefore, we are seeking to accomplish something unknown. Another approach is to ask, "If this happened in a person's life, what would be different?" or, "If this shaped our congregation, how would our congregation be different?"[3]

EVALUATION AS A TOOL FOR LEADING, NOT REPORTING[4]

When conversations turn to the need to define results and outcomes, many people think that such efforts are designed only to set a standard by which success can be measured at the end of a project. That is one use of outcomes, but it is not the primary one. The most important benefit of defining the purpose or outcome for every activity is that the desired outcome can shape every aspect of the planning and execution of the activity.

If one is planning a choir retreat, for example, the temptation is to make a list of possible locations, suggested dates, options for guest leaders, and activities for the weekend. Instead, the starting point is to gain clarity about what will be different at the end of the retreat. What is the change the leaders are seeking? How does the mission of the congregation shape the hopes for the retreat? What outcomes are desired? That exercise alone will guide and give focus to all the planning for the retreat and how those plans are carried out.

One of the myths of American industry is that Henry Ford invented the assembly line, which then permitted him to build a car that could be sold for $500, an amount that large numbers of working people could afford. The reality is just the reverse. Ford determined that $500 was the most that large numbers of people could pay for a car, and inventing the assembly line was the only way he could devise to accomplish that task.

He determined that the task was not just to build a car but to build a car in such a way *so that* it could be sold for $500; only then did he unlock the manufacturing plan required to accomplish such a goal. So it is with ministries.

There is often resistance to the whole notion of results in ministry settings, as if to focus on results takes something away from the creativity or faithfulness of our work. The opposite is actually the case. By giving attention to accomplishments, we will tend to channel our efforts in the most beneficial ways for those we seek to serve. Many of the results we seek are complex and ambiguous at times, which is all the more reason we must seek to clarify them so that our planning can have clarity as well.

Our focus on defining outcomes does not suggest that the goals or results we name and toward which we plan are the *only* results that will emerge as we carry out our plans. The Spirit works in and among us and may multiply the outcomes far beyond "all we can ask or imagine," as Ephesians reminds us (3:20).

FRUITFULNESS AS AN ALTERNATIVE TO SUCCESS

Clergypersons sometimes feel that they have only two options: one is "faithfulness," with little regard for results, and the other is to adopt the "success" culture they see around them. But a third option is fruitfulness. Success is not the goal of pastoral leadership, but fruitfulness is. Fruitfulness always holds within it the important passion for faithfulness, for no genuine and lasting fruitfulness is possible without such faithfulness. But fruitfulness also captures a comparable passion for accomplishments repeatedly referenced in the Bible as *fruits*.

Fruitfulness is vastly different from what the world regards as success. Fruitfulness has as its goal not personal advancement or acclaim but the advancement of God's reign on earth. It seeks to shape the life and work of the congregation through a shared passion for its mission. Fruitful leaders care about results because results are ways to go beyond merely *filling* a pastoral role to active participation in seeking results that we are convinced emerge from the gospel we preach.

CHAPTER ONE

A BIBLICAL MANDATE FOR FRUITFULNESS

We believe that the Bible begins and ends with an image of fruitfulness and that Scripture throughout leads us to conclude that churches, as the body of Christ on earth, are intended by God to be fruitful.

The image of fruitfulness fit the biblical world, so dominated as it was by agriculture. The richness of all that is embodied in this concept was familiar to those hearing calls that they "bear fruit" (Matthew 3:8; John 15:8). They quickly got the point that good trees bear good fruit and bad trees cannot bear good fruit (Matthew 7:18; Luke 6:43). Comparing the expectation that disciples will bear fruit to the experience of good seed sown in good soil producing a good harvest fit their world (Mark 4:20; Luke 8:15). The images of pruning and destroying unproductive trees would not have been lost on them (Matthew 7:19; Luke 3:9; John 15:2). And they certainly would have understood the difference between the vine and the branches and the reminder that "the branch cannot bear fruit by itself unless it abides in the vine." So they could understand the promise that those "who abide in me and I in them bear much fruit" (John 15:4-5).

FRUITFULNESS AS PART OF GOD'S CHARACTER

We begin the conversation about fruitfulness as the goal of church leadership with the question of the *will of God* for the church's ministry. A basis for discerning God's will is found in considering the *nature of God*. Fruitfulness is an aspect of *God's character*.

In Genesis we quickly discover that God is creative and productive.

1

As the stars and planets are spun into existence out of the void, God populates the earth with beings of every kind. When humans are created, they are invited to reflect the nature of their Creator with the command to "be fruitful and multiply" (1:22). The Bible shows God to be a being of movement and resourcefulness.

The Bible consistently states God's desires and expectations in terms of fruitfulness. Look up the word *fruit* in a concordance. The word appears more than 150 times. *Fruitful* appears nearly 30 times. One would assume that its use would typically have to do with people eating fruit or having children. When you examine the texts, however, you discover so much more. Let us consider three types of fruitfulness that God hopes we will display.

THE FRUIT OF GOD'S EXPANDING REIGN

Notice how the term *fruitful* is used in the conversation between God and Abram as the Lord changes his name to Abraham and offers to be in a covenant relationship with him:

> I will make you very fruitful; I will make nations of you, and kings will come from you. I will establish my covenant as an everlasting covenant between me and you and your descendants after you for the generations to come, to be your God and the God of your descendants after you. (Genesis 17:6-7 NIV)

Fruitful in this context points to the offspring that God plans for Abraham and Sarah. It also relates to the blessings brought to their lives by being in covenant with God. This covenant includes the promises of land and the assurance of God's provision for their needs. The other side of the covenant assumes that Abraham and Sarah will be fruitful for God as well. They will be obedient to the Lord, remain in relationship with God, and raise their offspring in such a way that the covenant will endure from generation to generation. The intention of God for Abraham's fruitfulness is repeated later in Genesis when the Lord shares plans to destroy Sodom. In Genesis 18:18, the Lord states, "Abraham will surely become a great and powerful nation, and all nations on earth will be blessed through him" (NIV).

Here God is stating the expectation that the fruitfulness of Abraham and Sarah's way of life will be a blessing to others. It is the Lord's desire to bless Abraham and Sarah. However, the greater purpose of this covenant is to plant the seeds of God's goodness in the barrenness that comes to those who do not know the Lord. Abraham and Sarah, through the doorway of their covenant, enter what later portions of the Bible will call the reign of God. Their task is to open this door to others and extend the blessings of the covenant to those around them as well.

In Exodus, when the covenant is presented to Moses on Mount Sinai, God restates the intention that Israel is to have a unique role in the world as a nation of priests. The idea is that a people made holy through their covenant with God will enable all the nations of the world to be blessed in like fashion. This type of fruitfulness, first found in the covenant with Abraham and Sarah, is a thread that runs throughout the Bible. The hope of God is clearly that the covenant people will widen the circle by inviting others to know the Lord as they do. This theology of God's expanding realm underpins Jesus' commandment: "Therefore go and make disciples of all nations, baptizing them in the name of the Father and of the Son and of the Holy Spirit, and teaching them to obey everything I have commanded you. And surely I am with you always, to the very end of the age" (Matthew 28:19-20 NIV).

In the Revelation of John, we find a vision of heaven in which all of God's blessings are fully enjoyed by the nations of the earth: "Then the angel showed me the river of the water of life. . . . On each side of the river stood the tree of life, bearing twelve crops of fruit, yielding its fruit every month. And the leaves of the tree are for the healing of the nations" (22:1-2 NIV).

This is a vision of the reign of God in its fullest. In the Revelation of John, it is not a hoped-for event or a hastily glimpsed image. It is the reality in which the children of God live. In Revelation, the fruit of Abraham's covenant, the fulfilled great commission with the church as the new Israel, is fully shared with everyone who needs to "taste and see that the LORD is good" (Psalm 34:8a).

Although Christ never used the term *fruitful* in the Great Commission, it is evident that his desire was for his disciples to share the fruit of God's promises with others.

THE FRUIT OF RIGHTEOUSNESS

In Psalms and Proverbs, the fruit of a life surrendered to God is expressed in the transformed character of the person. To know the Lord

3

is to become holy, or righteous. The author of Psalm 1 speaks with great joy about persons who reflect the character of God in their lives:

> Happy are those
>> who do not follow the advice of the wicked,
> or take the path that sinners tread,
>> or sit in the seat of scoffers;
> but their delight is in the law of the LORD,
>> and on his law they meditate day and night.
> They are like trees
>> planted by streams of water,
> which yield their fruit in its season,
>> and their leaves do not wither.
> In all that they do, they prosper. (vv. 1-3)

The fruit yielded by those who follow the Lord is in sharp contrast to the fruitless existence of those who live contrary to God's commands.

Proverbs reinforces this concept by focusing our attention on what happens in our lives when we fall in love with the wisdom of God. The voice of Wisdom beckons the reader,

> I love those who love me,
>> and those who seek me find me.
> With me are riches and honor,
>> enduring wealth and prosperity.
> My fruit is better than fine gold;
>> what I yield surpasses choice silver. (8:17-19 NIV)

Proverbs states that when God's wisdom is integrated into our lives, it bears fruit in our character. The transformed life, guided by the counsel of God and the sound judgment arising from the mind of the believer, is a fruit that bears fruit. The seeds encased in God's righteousness, planted in the fertile soil of the believer's life, give rise to healthy relationships, sound vocational decisions, and a stewardship of goals and possessions that bless generation after generation.

This transformation is not simply about fruit that benefits individual lives. It is to affect the broader society. Proverbs shares the Lord's hatred of pride and arrogance, the basis for self-centered behavior that often harms others. The fruit of righteousness curtails evil behavior and perverse speech. A society void of such things would have less sensational evening news reports but would truly be a better place to live.

The passage continues to show how society as a whole is blessed when rulers display the fruit of God's wisdom by creating just laws and governing in ways that benefit all rather than a few:

> By me kings reign
> and rulers make laws that are just;
> by me princes govern,
> and all nobles who rule on earth. (8:15-16 NIV)

Throughout Proverbs, we find the calling to honest business, fair practices with others, consistency in speech, generosity, and care of spouse and children. In the last two verses of Proverbs 8 we find a summation of the value of the fruit of God's wisdom in our lives:

> For whoever finds me finds life
> and obtains favor from the LORD;
> but those who miss me injure themselves;
> all who hate me love death. (vv. 35-36)

Leaders often measure the strength of the churches they serve by the scope of the churches' ministries. This overlooks the greater impact that the church is having in its community through the ethical conduct and sound decision making of its members as they live daily in the world. Formed in Christ, these members undertake a variety of vocational pursuits: teachers, doctors, farmers, lawyers, laborers, scientists, managers, and business owners. They touch most sectors of the economy, including business, government, the military, and nonprofits. The righteous life they pursue has a ripple effect across the culture in which they live.

Years ago Tom went to buy a used car from John and Kay, a married couple who were members of a church he served. Often people go to buy a used car with fear and trepidation. Like attorneys, politicians, and, yes, pastors, used car salesmen are often the punch line of jokes that characterize them as shady and unscrupulous. John and Kay, however, enjoyed a reputation in the community as people who were honest and fair.

> When I stopped by their dealership and began to discuss a particular car with John, I knew I did not need to fear being sold a bad vehicle or paying too high a price. Long before CarMax made no-haggle car sales popular, John and Kay were selling cars by simply saying, "Tom, we're going to give you our best price for this car."

I knew I could trust John and Kay, not because of their friendship or because I was their pastor, but because John and Kay were so deeply formed by the teaching of the church. The beauty of the righteous life is that it removes anxiety from every aspect of our lives. When John and Kay offered their price, I knew that it was a price fair to the customer and fair to them as the owners of a business. Buying a car without fear of hidden problems or the anxiety that the price is too high is a blessing.

One of the key reasons that Christian leaders want churches to grow is the benefit that will come to our communities when more people like John and Kay own businesses, work in the government, and provide leadership to their community. Such people enrich our society. They have learned Jesus' secret of being in the world but not of the world. While they live and work in our community, they uphold the standard of God's reign in the way they conduct their lives.

Church leaders must understand what is at stake when their congregations no longer influence their neighbors and communities as they once did. The transformative effect of Christ on people is a blessing to spouse, children, vocation, and the influence each person has on the larger society.

The New Testament invites us to consider that for people to exhibit the righteousness of God, they will need to find personal transformation through a relationship with Jesus Christ. In the Gospels, Jesus uses the images of fruit and fruitfulness several times to inform his followers that such transformation is not possible until we find life in him. The image of the vine and the branches in the Gospel of John is a vivid metaphor related to the need of the follower to be fully connected to Christ if he or she is to find transformation. Losing this connection is to risk losing the life and power of Christ that make the transformed life possible.

Paul uses similar imagery in Romans 11 when he describes the way the Gentiles, as a "wild olive shoot," have been grafted into the vine, among those already there. The purpose of this grafting is so that they can be transformed as they are nourished by the root, Christ. Without such a relationship with Christ, there is no possibility of being transformed. Once this new life in Christ is found, Colossians states that Christ's followers are to be productive for the Lord: "We pray this in order that you may live a life worthy of the Lord and may please him in every way: bearing fruit in every good work" (1:10 NIV).

THE FRUIT OF JUSTICE

The Bible calls God's people to live in a state of justice that far exceeds occasional moments of compassion or generosity. The call for justice is the expectation of God that all people will find adequate resources to enjoy life. Throughout the Prophets, metaphors related to the fruitfulness of God's realm are employed to help the people of Israel understand that the character of God demands fairness in the administration of civil law and integrity in matters of economics. The prophets believed that those of greater power and wealth should address the poverty experienced by some of God's people. They attempted to remove anxiety by reminding Israel that in God's realm, there is a sufficient abundance of resources to supply everyone's needs:

> Is not this the kind of fasting I have chosen:
> to loose the chains of injustice
>   and untie the cords of the yoke,
> to set the oppressed free
>   and break every yoke?
> Is it not to share your food with the hungry
>   and to provide the poor wanderer with shelter—
> when you see the naked, to clothe him,
>   and not to turn away from your own flesh and blood? (Isaiah 58:6-7 NIV)

It is particularly offensive when these resources are hoarded by the few rather than enjoyed by the many. Having provided such abundance, God is angered upon seeing vast disparity among people. It is particularly upsetting to God when injustice has been committed in order to gain wealth and resources. The prophets spend whole chapters communicating God's disgust for those who exploit the poor, misuse the court system to get what they want, or gain their wealth through the misuse of power. Likewise, the ire of God is raised when a nation of priests fails to remember the Lord's clear expectation to defend the basic rights of poor and vulnerable people. God, whose nature finds joy in justice, does not take lightly such a sin of omission. Jeremiah employs a metaphor of obesity when he speaks this word of judgment. Here the people are guilty of gorging themselves on God's fruitfulness while letting their neighbors starve:

7

Like cages full of birds,
   their houses are full of deceit;
they have become rich and powerful
   and have grown fat and sleek.
Their evil deeds have no limit;
      they do not plead the case of the fatherless to win it,
      they do not defend the rights of the poor.
(Jeremiah 5:27-28 NIV)

Ezekiel employs this same metaphor of hoarding rather than sharing God's fruitfulness in explaining the hardship that comes to those who ignore God's justice: "Now this was the sin of your sister Sodom: She and her daughters were arrogant, overfed and unconcerned; they did not help the poor and needy" (Ezekiel 16:49 NIV).

Isaiah 3–5 is perhaps one of the clearest examples of the use of fruitfulness as a biblical metaphor for God's expectations of the covenant people. In Isaiah 3:14, the prophet proclaims that the chosen people were to be a vineyard whose fruit would bless all people. Instead, their blatant injustice destroyed the potential of fruitfulness. They used their social and economic advantage to profit from the poor whom God would have them bless. The prophet warns that it was not in the nature of God to turn a blind eye to injustice:

The LORD enters into judgment
   against the elders and leaders of his people:
"It is you who have ruined my vineyard;
   the plunder from the poor is in your houses.
What do you mean by crushing my people
   and grinding the faces of the poor?"
      declares the Lord, the LORD Almighty.
(Isaiah 3:14-15 NIV)

The Lord employs the image of fruitfulness to convey disappointment that the covenant people, having enjoyed so much, share so little. God's judgment is recorded in "The Song of the Vineyard" in Isaiah 5. Here the Lord talks about the joy of lovingly planting a vineyard that would bless others, only to discover that it instead produced bad fruit. The nation of Judah, through its disregard for the poor and vulnerable, is like a vineyard that will be torn down because of its failure to produce good fruit:

"Now I will tell you
what I am going to do to my vineyard:
I will take away its hedge,
and it will be destroyed;
I will break down its wall,
and it will be trampled.
I will make it a wasteland,
neither pruned nor cultivated,
and briers and thorns will grow there.
I will command the clouds
not to rain on it."
The vineyard of the LORD Almighty
is the house of Israel,
and the men of Judah
are the garden of his delight.
And he looked for justice, but saw bloodshed;
for righteousness, but heard cries of distress. (Isaiah 5:5-7 NIV)

If God felt so strongly that the people of Judah bear the fruit of justice in their society, certainly the Lord anticipates the same from the
church today. Jesus' call to be "the light of the world" (Matthew 5:14)
in the Sermon on the Mount includes the desire of God for the church
to be fruitful as it cares for the poor and advocates for the weak in the
broader society. Like a vineyard that God has planted to bless all who
live in the community, the church is to be a place of provision and a
place of joy. When congregational leaders see their church as a vineyard
whose fruit was planted to enrich the community, they will act in ways
that will bless others as a way of life instead of an occasional special
event. When we embrace the community sufficiently to see that there
are many forms of despair in which people live, we will no longer argue
about whether the church is called to a fruitful ministry. We will be
compelled to dream, plan, and strategize for ways the church can be productive for God and a blessing for those who do not know the goodness
of God's promises.

AND DON'T FORGET PRUNING

Bishop Robert Schnase tells of teaching on fruitfulness in a congregation. He recounted many of the Scripture verses about fruitfulness
with their images of vines, branches, seedtime, harvest, soils, vineyards,

trees, and fruits. As he was listing these agricultural metaphors, someone from the audience shouted out, "Don't forget pruning!"[1] Pruning is as much a part of a fruitful harvest as is planting.

Management pioneer Peter Drucker often used the phrase "creative abandonment" to describe the process by which people and organizations determine what they should stop doing. In most organizations new programs are added on to everything else currently being done. Hardly ever do people stop to ask, "What will we discontinue to make room for the new effort?" They seem to assume new undertakings can be accomplished without undermining current programs or diluting the focus of the organization.

For a time, this process can be sustained. Over the long term, however, the proliferation of new endeavors, without "pruning," creates unhealthy results, for any organization has a limited amount of time, energy, and resources. Therefore, it is crucial to make judgments constantly regarding how we use our resources to fulfill our mission so that we are a genuinely mission-shaped congregation.

Creative abandonment provides the opportunity to ask periodically, "What can we stop doing without compromising our mission?" When people brainstorm about such possibilities, many good ideas emerge. After reviewing the implications and impact, they discover that pruning some branches will turn out to be quite workable. Many of the things may seem to be small, but every activity takes time, energy, and resources that cannot be devoted to other efforts.

Do you have ministries that are like the tree Jesus mentioned that did not bear fruit and needed to be cut down?

THE BIBLICAL CALL FOR FRUITFULNESS

Throughout Scripture, we have seen, God calls the covenant people to live lives of fruitfulness. We are to labor for the advance of God's reign, for righteousness to be normative to the human character, and for justice to bless everyone. Just as in the past, God intends for the covenant people of today to be fruitful and make disciples in response to the grace we know in Christ Jesus. The promise remains: "And surely I am with you always, to the very end of the age" (Matthew 28:20 NIV).

10

CHAPTER TWO

AN INVITATION TO LABOR FOR GOD'S HARVEST

The good news is that God invites us to be a part of fruitful ministry. Winchester, Virginia, where Tom grew up, is surrounded by apple orchards. It is known as the Apple Capital of the World, and the yearly Apple Blossom Festival is a celebration of fruitfulness. A casual observer may think that the bountiful harvest just happens on its own. But residents of Winchester know that the fruitfulness of the apple trees depends on the care and attention of orchard workers. They tend the trees all year long—putting spacers in the branches, fertilizing, pruning, and spraying the trees—so that every fall the orchards will be laden with fruit.

The realm of God is like those apple orchards, and we are the laborers responsible for reaping a plentiful harvest. For churches to be fruitful congregations, pastors and laypersons must take their roles seriously. They must learn to look at congregations with the eye of the fruit grower who longs for God's word to go forth to all and who yearns for the time when righteousness and justice will flourish in every land.

THE MISSION: TO GATHER A PLENTIFUL HARVEST

The fruit grower is not likely to be in doubt about the mission. All the labor is directed toward a bountiful harvest of apples each year. A primary question we must ask is whether we as clergy, lay leaders, and congregations are as clear about our mission and how it shapes our work.

The words *mission* and *vision* are common in the vocabulary of the church. Church leaders, speakers, and writers use them generously and define them differently, but they are crucial if we are going to be fruitful leaders. Otherwise, we do not know what we are seeking as God's covenant people and do not recognize who and what we are called to be and do. We are then unlikely to be among those who are helping advance the reign of God in our time.

For the purposes of this book, we define *mission* as what we exist *to do*, why we exist. Denominations and many congregations, as well as other organizations, have an overarching mission. The denomination of which we are a part says, "The mission of the Church is to make disciples of Jesus Christ for the transformation of the world." Congregations often have a mission that is similar: "To share God's love"; "To take the gospel to all people"; or "To serve those in need." Such a mission is intended to shape the ministry of that part of Christ's church.

The mission statements of Christian congregations are often similar. That is not surprising since they share a common Scripture, and many have a common understanding of the gospel. The mission statement of a congregation can remain the same for a long time as well.

To Change the World

I was preaching on God's mission ... and then moved on to a more specific focus—talking about how the church is the body of Christ in the world today, sent on the same mission Jesus Christ was sent on. And how when we lose sight of that mission and start focusing on other things, we lose our connection to God and become just another social organization among many.

I then put it to the congregation like this. "If someone came up to you this week and asked you, 'Why does your church exist,' what would you say?" The responses were slow to start off, but they began to come after a while. "To connect people together." "To share the love of God with others." "To offer Christ to people."

And then, in a quiet but confident ten-year-old voice from the middle of the room: **"To change the world."**

The Holy Spirit was thick in the room at that moment. Whispers could be heard as the grown-ups asked one another who had brought

> the sermon to a halt with a burst of Holy Spirit–inspired truth. Because for a few moments there I literally could not go on. The sermon was irrelevant, insignificant fluff. Power had been spoken aloud, and I did not know how to proceed. What more needs to be said when a ten-year-old believes that his church exists to change the world?[1]
>
> Andy Bryan

Along with their mission, congregations have a set of values. These may be explicit, and you will find them on a church bulletin or website: We are loving and inclusive, or warm and hospitable, compassionate and justice minded. Even if they are not written down, each congregation has values that shape how they live out their mission.

Values describe your church at its best. They are written for two reasons. First, they describe who you really are. They help someone interested in your church discover the personality of your congregation by reading short descriptive phrases or sentences. A church that is the most joyful when it is serving homeless persons in its community and that invests time and money to do so each week should write a value statement that communicates its heart for the poor to the community. A congregation that is in a neighborhood in transition and has decided to welcome and embrace diversity rather than flee from the situation should write a value statement regarding the joy found in valuing persons of various backgrounds.

These value statements have the power to solidify community identity for members and draw persons not yet involved into the life of these congregations. Value statements have the ability to overcome the homogeneity found in most churches around appearance and socioeconomic factors by attracting people on the basis of shared beliefs and a common theology of what the church is called to be. No church can be all things. Value statements clarify what makes a church distinctive. They spell out the congregation's particular areas of interest and focus within the larger ecclesiology common to other churches.

Second, value statements define what a congregation strives to be. There are times when it is very helpful to write down what you want to be so that you can understand what you hope to become. A church with a long history of segregation in a community that is racially divided may write down a value related to honoring diversity because members need

13

to remind themselves of who they long to be in the present and future. This can be especially powerful when leaders desire a future that is in some way a radical departure from the past. In this case, the value is a statement of intended transformation. There would be plans and goals written to enable the congregation to reach the intended future state described in the value.

Some congregations add many of their values to their mission statement, which is not helpful. Doing this will simply confuse the line between "being" and "doing." Values mingled with a mission statement sometimes tell a great deal about how they want to be but may not offer clarity about what they exist *to do*.

That is why we also speak of the importance of *vision*. Vision is what we are called to do *now* and *in this particular place*—given our mission, the values and strengths of our people, and the needs of those around us. (We note that some use the word *vision* to speak of the overarching purpose that we call *mission*, and use *mission* for the more specific calling in this time and place. The choice of words is not significant as long as the concepts are clear.)

Later we will discuss what can only be described as a "God-sized vision" that has helped shape the life of Floris United Methodist Church. First, we will look at fruitful leadership in terms of living toward the mission and accomplishing toward the mission.

BUSY: NOT NECESSARILY FRUITFUL

What does fruitfulness look like?

A common confusion is equating fruitfulness with expanding programs and activities. The question is not, "Are we doing more?" but, "Are we accomplishing more?" It is a question of outcomes rather than activity. Organizations, including churches, are not ends in themselves. Everything exists for the *mission*, and the mission, along with values, shapes everything.

Perhaps the most important task for a leader is, first, to be sure that there *is* a mission that everyone knows and shares. Then the leader must keep everyone focused on the mission and thus be sure that all the organization does is directed toward the fulfillment of that mission. So the ultimate focus must always be not on what we are *doing* but on what we are *accomplishing toward the mission*. Are we bearing fruit? And is it good fruit?

A common problem among churches, as well as other organizations, is that there tends to be a gravitational pull toward activity-focused measurement rather than on results. And we also are likely to lean toward a focus on internal operations and services rather than an external focus on those the church exists to reach and serve.

Therefore, if we are not paying attention to outcomes, it is likely that no one, including the congregation as a whole, is being held accountable for results called for by the mission. "Over the years I've come to see that few people are being measured for the right things," says Sue Mallory.[2] What people do, how they spend their time, and how resources are allocated should be shaped by the outcomes we seek. And the outcomes are shaped by the mission.

The goal is always to stay focused on the mission and core values and to stay clear about how the outcomes of any project grow out of the mission and values. Once we do this, people will understand the significance and rationale for each particular program or project. That is far more compelling than what we often do—tell the congregation what we are going to do or tell them what we want *them* to do—without the *why*. Leaders gain credibility when they make sure that everyone sees that their motivation in any endeavor is the achievement of *mission results—is mission shaped*—rather than advancing a personal priority or desire.

EVALUATE ON OUTCOMES

The dilemma is that typically when staff do not know what they are to produce, or when staff do not know what they are being held accountable to produce, they tend to value and measure their work by the amount of time consumed or the number of tasks accomplished. We all have been in supervision meetings with staff or evaluation meetings with personnel committees where a person's work was measured by how many hours was spent doing the work or how many visits, phone calls, reports, dollars, or volunteers were involved. The number of hours, visits, calls, reports, and so on is not a measure of what is *produced* in ministry but rather a measure of what is *expended* in ministry. Without a clear and shared outcome in place for a staff person's work, it is impossible to judge if the expenditure of hours, activities, and resources was appropriate or effective. The

real issue of hours and resources is not whether they were spent but whether they moved the congregation toward the outcome of ministry to which it is called by its mission. Staff members are not paid to work hard, but to achieve ministry.[3]
Gil Rendle and Susan Beaumont

WHAT OUTCOMES ARE WE SEEKING?

The first step in naming outcomes is to determine what things are most critical to your mission. What *is* the mission of the congregation? What is the change you seek? What do you want to be different? What are the outcomes called for by the mission?

Another way to think about this is to ask, "What would be different if the mission were accomplished?" Such thinking is not easy, but it is essential in order to move from merely managing resources and activities to leading toward outcomes. The temptation is to move immediately to focus on the process, procedures, or activities. It is wise to resist that temptation. Stay with a focus upon the outcomes desired until everyone understands and can confirm them.

"To use the language of fruitfulness," says Bishop Robert Schnase, "causes congregations to become clearer about desired outcomes. . . . Fruitfulness directs our focus to what we accomplish for God's purposes and corrects the tendency to congratulate ourselves for all the work, resources, and people we apply to a task while ignoring or denying that our efforts may be making little difference."[4]

FRUITFUL LEADERSHIP IS PURPOSEFUL

The other day, I was driving home from Dulles airport. I was not in the best mood. My plane was small and late. I had to walk a mile to get my car. I was tired, worried, and in heavy traffic. And then, I looked to the left and noticed the field of flowers planted on the median strip. You see them along roadways all over the country.

The flowers are called "Cosmos." Well, something about them instantly transformed my mood, and I smiled. It wasn't just that they were so delicately pretty, it's that they were so random, so "off-the-page," so gratuitously beautiful. And I wondered: How many lives have been changed by those flowers? How many marriages have been saved, legal decisions re-thought, bills re-drafted, wars averted by this "Visitation of the Cosmos" on the Dulles access road? Stranger things have happened.

And I realized how really very purposeful they are. Plants do not produce flowers for their own sake. A very intelligent God designed an evolutionary process whereby the shape and color of the Cosmos please the birds and the bees. They work hard to do this. They are also sacrificial. Indeed, an annual like the Cosmos dies in the process of bearing this fruit, lifting the flower high in the sky so that the seeds might fall into their beds and a brand new field might thrive next summer. I thought: "A flower is a plant on a mission."

That caused me to think about my work. I am busy, but in my sane moments, I remember that it isn't hard to be busy. "Busy" is not an end in itself. Weeds are busy, cancer is busy. I can easily fall into the trap of thinking I am a success if I am busy, if I am working hard. But I considered the Cosmos, and I longed for that way of being where everything I do is meaningful, where I am in the flow; that blessed state where I am on a mission and my work is bearing fruit.[5]
David McAllister-Wilson

ACCOUNTABILITY

When our efforts toward God's purposes are making little difference, no matter how busy we are, we are neither fruitful nor faithful. And as church leaders, we are called to be both.

"When I hear Jesus say that 'I appointed you to go and bear fruit,' a word occurs to me: accountability," says Kenneth H. Carter Jr. "Sometimes accountability can be measured, and sometimes it cannot be measured. What is important is that we allow the grace of God to be poured out through us. We allow the inward and spiritual grace to become an outward and visible sign."[6]

The fruit grower knows what it is to be *accountable* for the harvest and does all that is possible to ensure a plentiful crop. The outward and visible sign is very clear when the harvest comes. This sounds similar to the work of the steward we find in Scripture and can help us see the significance of accountability for fruitful leaders.

The steward in biblical times was a household administrator, but the role was never one of mere caretaking for what is. As we appropriate the language of steward for the church in our time, we not only note that it means more than a caretaker. It is *more* in that the steward always labors on behalf of the gospel. The work of the steward is to be Spirit filled and infused by God's vision. Stewards are actively moving toward God's intended harvest and moving others along as well. There is a major difference between a caretaker and an active steward laboring in God's vineyard. Thus, the word *steward* captures much of the spirit of fruitful leadership.

Indeed, Hans Conzelmann reminds us that the metaphor of steward in 1 Corinthians holds together faithfulness and fruitfulness. The metaphor makes the specific point of faithfulness, he says, and makes clear that stewards are accountable for what they do.[7]

Fruitfulness is a biblical way of talking about such accountability. It is a way of saying that we are responsible to see that *what is intended* grows into *what is accomplished*, that the dream of a rich harvest actually becomes that rich harvest. While we never forget that God gives the growth, we also know that, like the fruit grower, we are *accountable* for planting and watering (1 Corinthians 3:6). We are called to bear fruit and hence are accountable for the fruits of ministry.

For John Wesley also, "fruits of ministry" was a key concept. He liked to ask three questions of spiritual leaders: (1) Have they faith? (2) Have they gifts? and (3) Have they fruit?[8] Wesley's attention to fruits was one factor that led him to permit women and other laypeople to preach, even though he shared reservations common in his time about their preaching. He saw the obvious fruit of such preaching as evidence that it was of God.

Fruitful leadership, then, is leadership that shapes itself around accomplishing the mission. We have found that two words consistently help us stay focused on the mission of anything we do, no matter how small or large: *so that*. Indeed, we believe these may be the two most powerful words you will learn from this book.

THE TWO MOST POWERFUL WORDS FOR FRUITFUL LEADERSHIP: *SO THAT*

The biblical mandate for fruitfulness is clear. We are accountable for accomplishing outcomes that move us toward the mission. We also know that church leaders are called to be faithful *and* fruitful.

But we often find ourselves mired in the endless managerial tasks that can seem far removed from bearing fruit. A first step is to find a way to redeem the ongoing tasks of ministry from operational necessities to arenas of fruitfulness. Two words are central to the task: *so that*. Those who learn to use these words well find that virtually everything they attempt begins with a concern for the fruit of the proposed effort.

BIBLICAL EXAMPLES

> Have them make me a sanctuary, so that I may dwell among them.
> (Exodus 25:8)

The pattern is familiar. A new church sees the possibility of reaching more people for Christ by constructing a church building. Or a growing congregation envisions a new educational building to help more children and youth grow in their faith. There are passion and energy about the possibilities. Members of the congregation begin to make plans and project costs. From that moment, what had previously been a focus on the *purpose* of the new building now becomes a discussion almost exclusively about the new building. Everyone will be preoccupied with whether to build, whether to build now or later, the cost of the project, interest rates, and a host of other legitimate issues. How did it happen that the building receives 90 percent of the attention when the church never set out to build a building but set out to reach more people for Christ or help children and youth grow in their faith?

Without leadership, the people of the congregation will begin to think that the church is about building a new structure. Not so. The church is not in the building business. The church is in the discipleship business, and in this case, the church has discerned that they must have more space to fulfill that mission—*so that* they can reach more people for Christ.

Having a clear *so that* statement helps to keep everyone focused on the end and not just the means. The purpose of "making a sanctuary" in the Exodus passage is plain: so that the Lord may dwell among them. Building the sanctuary is not an end in itself. The challenge is whether the people can stay focused on the purpose—the *so that*—whether it is in Exodus times or in our own day.

In the same way, let your light shine before others, so that they may see your good works and give glory to your Father in heaven. (Matthew 5:16)

Jesus calls his followers to let their light shine before others. Humility might cause Christians to be reluctant to appear as if they are doing good things for public viewing. But the *so that* reveals the purpose of such action—that others "may see your good works and give glory to your Father in heaven." Letting others see the light from our lives means little in and of itself. It finds its meaning as a way of linking others to God's love.

Do not be conformed to this world, but be transformed by the renewing of your minds, so that you may discern what is the will of God—what is good and acceptable and perfect. (Romans 12:2)

The Bible calls Christians to be different. Paul's exhortation not to be conformed to the world is one of many admonitions for faithful Christians not to mimic the ways of the world. Throughout eras of church history, Christians from various traditions have approached

20

nonconformity in multiple ways, and there is always a temptation for the difference to be an end in itself. Those who insist on clothing or hair styles that cause them immediately to stand out as different make a certain statement. However, Paul's use of *so that* to advocate nonconformity keeps the focus on the purpose of the nonconformity. Having different standards from the world is for discerning the will of God—the good and acceptable and perfect.

For God so loved the world that he gave his only Son, so that everyone who believes in him may not perish but may have eternal life. (John 3:16)

God's love was revealed among us in this way: God sent his only Son into the world so that we might live through him. (1 John 4:9)

These two passages capture perhaps the greatest *so that* statements of the Bible. In them we see not only God's action in Christ but also the ultimate purpose for our lives and the world.

SO THAT IN THE LIVES OF CONGREGATIONS

Lovett remembers well the first time he asked a group of church leaders to try a *so that* exercise. He chose something simple. In fact, he wondered if the illustration would be so simple that it would not make the point. He used vacation church school (VCS) as the test case since many churches have a vacation church school or vacation Bible school (VBS) each year.

The setting was an annual leadership institute held by a major teaching church. In my workshop were just over one hundred people, about evenly divided between pastors and laity. To test that my example would work, I asked how many were familiar with a VCS or VBS. Everyone raised their hand. *This may be too easy*, I said to myself.

"I have an assignment for you," I continued. The assignment consisted of a simple sentence format:

I will do _____ so that _____ will happen.[1]

I invited each of them to complete the following sentence:

"Next summer our church will have a vacation church school so that…"

They began working. Soon I realized that few people were writing anything. They were looking around or staring at their paper. I could sense a level of struggle I had not anticipated. I was allowing much more time for the exercise than I had scheduled. When I realized that most were not completing the task, I called the group back together and acknowledged that the exercise seemed to be a bit difficult for some. I suggested that we ask the few people who had completed their sentence to share what they had done and then perhaps others could complete theirs.

The first volunteer reported: "Next summer our church will have a VCS so that the children of our church will experience a VCS." What do you say to that? Saying "thank you," I asked if there was another volunteer.

The second example offered was: "Next summer our church will have a VCS so that children will experience church as fun." My first thought was, *I'm not sure you need curriculum for that.*

Fearing that others would not be better, I asked if they would like to break into small groups to complete the task. They jumped at the opportunity not to try more on their own.

When it was time for the groups to report, most of the offerings were not appreciably different from the early individual ones. However, after a time there was one that captured well the purpose of the exercise. That statement was:

"Next summer our church will have a VCS so that the children of our church will come to know and love God more and that we will reach children in the community with God's love whom we have not reached before."

Thank goodness.

"Okay," I said to the group, "let's work with this one for a bit."

PLEASE BE OUR VACATION CHURCH SCHOOL DIRECTOR

For a moment, imagine that we did not have this *so that* statement. We simply knew we were going to have a VCS next summer just as we do every summer. Someone came to you months ahead of time and asked if you would consider serving as director for the coming summer's VCS, and let us assume you agreed to do so. You would probably think that your task was to put on a VCS. You likely would begin by addressing a series of tasks: setting a date, selecting curriculum, recruiting teachers, recruiting other volunteers for refreshments and activities, and so forth. Then you would conduct the VCS and follow up with the concluding details. Perhaps you would be invited to the church council to report on the VCS, and the group would express thanks to you and say they heard it was one of the best VCSs in recent years.

But now imagine a different scenario. This time the church has invested the time to discern their *so that* statement. Notice how *everything* changes. The invitation to serve is different. "Our church has discerned that God wants us to have a VCS next summer," the inviter tells you, "so that the children of our church will come to know and love God more and that we will reach children in the community with God's love whom we have not reached before. And we feel led to you as the person we would like to invite to direct this mission."

If you say yes to this request, you have agreed to something far different from the previous scenario. Before, you were asked to put on a VCS. This is an invitation of a different order.

Now, everything you might have done before needs rethinking. The *so that* must shape all decisions. For example, some of the people you would have invited to teach previously will no longer be the best choices. They could teach a VCS class, but they could not do what this *so that* would require them to do. And think about how other decisions may be altered based on this particular *so that*. It may determine whether the VCS should be in the daytime or evening, whether a fee can be charged or not, what curriculum you will choose, whom you must recruit as volunteers, where you will place the publicity, and whether the publicity will need to be in one language or multiple languages.

In other words, your assignment is no longer to direct a VCS; it is now to ensure that "the children of our church come to know and love God more and to reach children in the community with God's love whom we have not reached before."

A FOCUS ON ACTIVITIES AND NOT OUTCOMES

Now let us return to the group of one hundred clergy and laity attending the workshop. These are some of the most committed people around. They have a passion for their churches to be fruitful, or they would not be investing their time and money in traveling to a multiday teaching church institute. And they come from churches that have VCS every summer. But despite their dedication and their experience with VCSs in their churches, they were virtually stumped in coming up with a *so that* statement for this ministry that they do every year.

What does this mean? It probably means that they are having VCS without thinking about the change they seek by having VCS. They see VCS as an intrinsically good thing, and surely good things come from their efforts. But if there is no focus on the goals for VCS, then the task becomes simply to *have* VCS. The most important question becomes, "Did we have VCS this summer?" If the answer is, "Yes, we did," then everyone is likely to be satisfied.

What else do we do in churches each week without an effort to name the changes we are seeking through those ministries? We might ask, "Did we have church school this week?" But we are not asking, "Did church school this week accomplish what we discerned to be the outcome for which we established church school?"

We might ask, "Do we have a choir?" But we do not ask, "Is our choir accomplishing the outcome for which the choir exists?"

We might ask, "Did we have ushers last Sunday?" But we are not asking, "Did the ushers last Sunday do their work in such a way as to produce the outcome for which the usher ministry exists?"

We are not able to ask those more probing questions because we have not clearly established the purpose served by the most basic ministries of the church. Therefore, we are likely to spend our efforts on the activities without clarity concerning what God is calling us to accomplish through those activities. The activities were never intended to be ends in themselves, but that is what they tend to become. From the beginning, they were means to accomplish some change that God has called us to make.

TRANSFORMING ACTIVITIES TO OUTCOMES USING *SO THAT*

This is why many church activities operate on their own without a connection to the church's mission. This explains the frustration that many feel when, after all their work on a new mission statement, life goes on for worship, education, and finances just as it did before, with little, if any, connection to the new mission. This usually happens because there are so many parts of the church that function as silos, doing their work often very well but still not closely tied to the overall purpose of the congregation. Therefore, a congregation can waste much energy as it devotes time and effort without overall coordination and focus on the mission.

We now turn to the elements of a *so that* process for a congregation. We have developed a series of charts that some clergy and lay leaders have found useful as they work with this approach in their ministry settings. The charts are intended to be a tool to help churches focus on the steps of this process, but leaders in each congregation can best determine whether this kind of tool is the best approach in their setting. In any case, the charts help leaders see the intent of the *so that* process so they can discern how best to help their own congregations learn to ask the *so that* questions.

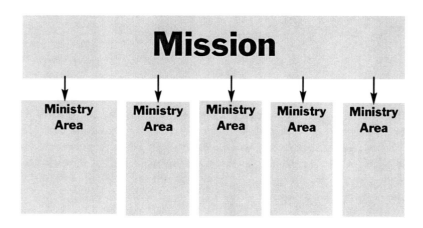

HOW ONE CHURCH BEGAN THE PROCESS

A *so that* process depends on a congregation having named its mission. Once that is done, you are in a position to plan for areas of congregational life that are set up to carry out the mission. We illustrate using one congregation's mission and how the *so that* process might apply to worship. Eventually, congregations can do comparable work for education, missions, stewardship, facilities—whatever their areas of ministry—so that all are mission shaped.

How did Trinity Church engage in the *so that* process for its worship ministry? Some time ago, the congregation had completed a process to name the mission of Trinity. It is a simple one and not different from the mission of many congregations: "To make disciples of Jesus Christ and serve others." But it has given the people of Trinity fresh energy and focus. The leaders in the congregation and many members can tell you the mission and what it means to them and their congregation. That step is in place, and many members are ready to work on next steps so the mission comes to life in all their ministries.

The mission of Trinity Church is to make disciples of Jesus Christ and to serve others.

Now they are preparing to discern a mission statement for their worship ministry. Imagine an afternoon retreat. The worship committee is there, along with the pastoral leadership of the congregation, the organist, and the choir director. They have invited a consultant who has worked with them the past year on their worship life. Also present are key laity who were passionate about the creation of their new mission statement and want to help find ways to live it out in all dimensions of the congregation's ministry.

One person begins by saying, "I always thought the mission of the worship ministry was to be sure we had high-quality worship every Sunday." Another responds, "But it needs to be connected with the church's mission statement we decided upon. Everything we do needs to be shaped by that overall mission." So they look back at that mission statement: "To make disciples of Jesus Christ and serve others." And then they begin brainstorming.

"What does worship have to do with making disciples? How? What does it look like?"

"And can worship affect our serving others? How could that happen in worship?"

"Why do we have worship anyway?"

After a time, the chair of the worship committee tests an idea: "The mission of the worship ministry is to communicate the gospel in word, song, and sight." Soon one of the pastors adds, "Maybe the mission is to make our worship a channel for the Holy Spirit to work among the people." At once, several in the group respond that maybe that is a good starting point, but it does not tell us much about what we are supposed to do.

They look at the *so that* chart. Maybe it could help. In the first box we could say: "The mission of the worship ministry is to make worship a channel for the Holy Spirit to work among the people."

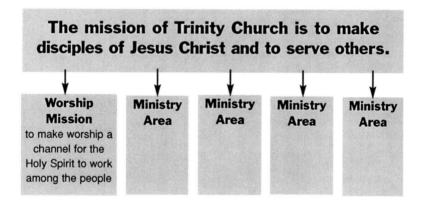

So that what?

So that the people hear the good news of Jesus Christ in ways they can receive with their minds and hearts.

So that, hearing the good news, they seek to become ever more faithful disciples, inviting others into discipleship and growing in service.

So that we live the mission of our church: To make disciples of Jesus Christ and serve others.

The group thought that was a good start: "At least we agree now that we are not here just to see that worship happens." Their mission with its related *so thats* will begin to shape their planning of worship. Asking the *so that* question in the worship ministry is likely to give focus to every part of that ministry and keep everything connected to the mission.

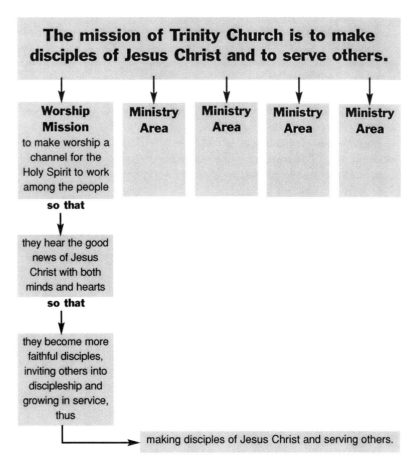

The mission of Trinity Church is to make disciples of Jesus Christ and to serve others.

Worship Mission
to make worship a channel for the Holy Spirit to work among the people

so that

they hear the good news of Jesus Christ with both minds and hearts

so that

they become more faithful disciples, inviting others into discipleship and growing in service, thus

Ministry Area

Ministry Area

Ministry Area

Ministry Area

making disciples of Jesus Christ and serving others.

Taking the Process to Another Level

Some areas of ministry have multiple components for which their own charts can be useful. Here is what a chart designed for the worship ministry might look like. Instead of the church's mission, this chart uses worship's mission, along with examples of the many components of worship. If the mission of the worship ministry is fulfilled, that directly contributes to the fulfillment of the congregational mission. The goal now is to make sure that every part of worship focuses on worship's mission and not just "doing our task."

Otherwise, the choir will think it is about being a choir. And ushers will think they are about being ushers. And the person who prepares the

28

bulletin will think it is about preparing a bulletin. Now they will see that the choir, ushers, and bulletin take on significance as they contribute to the mission of the worship ministry and, hence, to the mission of the church.

Trinity Church worked thoughtfully and prayerfully to develop their mission statement, and then those in the worship ministry spent an afternoon retreat working on what a mission statement for their ministry might be. They pushed one another to be clear about the *so thats* in order to sharpen their focus for their work.

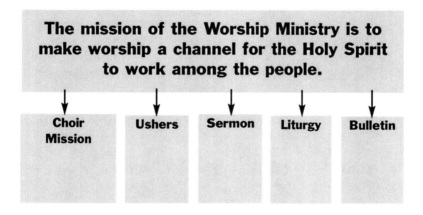

During that afternoon, their choir director and several choir members began to ask what this worship mission could mean for them. Just as a worship ministry and its mission are in place as one way to implement the congregation's mission, so the choir could work on its own mission and *so thats*.

The choir has a yearly retreat, and choir members always thought that was about having some fun and fellowship away from the church. But what if this year's retreat was *so that* we discern the mission of the choir? They would start with the mission of the church and then look at the mission and *so thats* of the worship ministry. It would be a chance to focus on what the choir *exists to do* in light of the other mission statements. That could change how they thought about their ministry.

Trinity Church had not thought about asking, "Why have a choir?" At the choir retreat, members and leaders began to engage that question. One can guess the initial answers to the questions:

"Well, we've always had a choir. Worship would not seem right without a choir."

"I cannot sing any longer in the symphony chorus, and this gives me a place to sing."

"Paying our soloists helps them get through graduate school, and maybe they will join our church."

The conversation took a different turn when the choir director and worship consultant talked about the worship ministry retreat and how they had developed a mission for the worship ministry. Choir members began to look at how their ministry might contribute to achieving the mission of the worship ministry and, hence, the mission of Trinity Church. They began to see that the life of the choir was going to look very different.

By the end of the retreat, they converted their work to a chart.

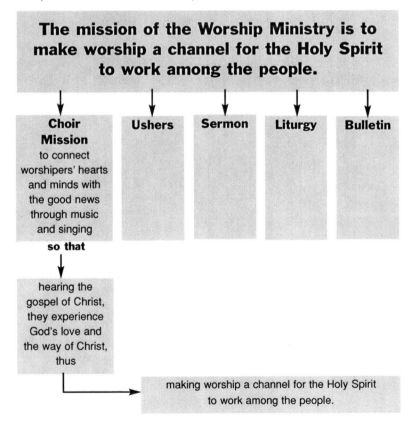

The mission of the Worship Ministry is to make worship a channel for the Holy Spirit to work among the people.

Choir	Ushers	Sermon	Liturgy	Bulletin

Mission
to connect worshipers' hearts and minds with the good news through music and singing

so that

hearing the gospel of Christ, they experience God's love and the way of Christ, thus

making worship a channel for the Holy Spirit to work among the people.

PRACTICAL IMPLICATIONS

Trinity Church's music program has always had a choir—for as long as anyone could remember. The church has done the things a church will usually do to have a choir, such as providing budget resources and having a volunteer and then a paid choir director. At times, the congregation has been very happy with the choir, and there were other times when it was the target of many complaints. As in other churches, when there were problems, the pastor and worship committee, along with the personnel committee, tried to correct the situation. So there was always a choir, and much of the time it made contributions to worship that the congregation appreciated. "We have a reputation in the community for having a good choir," they said proudly.

Now choir members can be part of something far larger than just "being in the choir." The choir director can now welcome members to choir practice by saying, "Thank you for coming. I know you love music, or you would not be here. But you are here for something more. You could find other ways to use your musical gifts, but you have chosen to come here not just to sing but to sing so that worshipers hear the gospel through music. We are all here to *connect worshipers' hearts and minds with God through singing and music.* And together with many others who contribute to the worship ministry, we are about *making worship a channel of the Holy Spirit to work among the people.*"

The choir then will begin practice with a prayer that the members may indeed be instruments of the Holy Spirit—and not performers. The director will choose music that helps worshipers hear the good news—but not just hear it. *It helps them hear it in ways they can receive with their minds and hearts.* New people have begun to attend worship, so the choir is now singing music they had not known before—music that some of the new people *can receive with their minds and hearts.*

Many significant results emerge through involving people in these exercises. Now choir members are on a mission with a vision of what they hope God will accomplish through them. Imagine how this might affect rehearsal attendance, punctuality before worship time, or the willingness to share special music for a Christmas cantata. The choir has the motivation to give their best when they sing. The director no longer needs to make rules about rehearsal attendance, on the one hand, or settle for poor performance, on the other.

Walking through the *so that* process, the director and choir members have entered into a sort of covenant together. Their willingness to sacrifice for the good of their weekly leadership in worship is inspired by their understanding of the mission to which God has called them. They are far more likely to sing well, prepare seriously, and recruit others to join them now that they have a clear understanding of their unique contributions to worship and discipleship in the life of the church. In short, they will begin to demonstrate the outcomes of a fruitful ministry because they fully acknowledge and embrace their mission. Such an exercise enables people to understand the great importance of their spiritual gifts and their unique function within the body of Christ.

And if the church needs to find a new choir director in the future, they will look for more than technical competence and credentials. They will seek someone who cares about learning what kind of music it is through which the congregation can receive the gospel with their minds and hearts—*so that* hearing the good news, they seek to become ever more faithful disciples, inviting others into discipleship and growing in service. So *that* we live the mission of our church: To make disciples of Jesus Christ and serve others.

ADAPTING *SO THAT* TO YOUR CONGREGATION

The *so that* process and *so that* charts are tools for helping leaders and congregations do their work in a way that they become more fully mission shaped. Some congregations have used the charts in ways that helped them focus in fresh ways on their mission. In other churches, such charts would not fit the culture, and even a formal *so that* process would not be well received. But leaders can have the *so that* concept in their own minds and can adapt it in ways that fit any congregation, no matter what its size or way of doing things.

Some find it helpful to use the *so that* process first for new ministries. For example, some younger single members may come to the pastor and suggest that "our church needs a singles ministry." The pastor might suggest that they talk with others and develop this *so that* sentence: "Our church will begin a singles ministry *so that*..." The ensuing give-and-take becomes a marvelous way to channel the new ministry in ways that fit the church's mission and the needs of singles.

Few groups can develop *so that* statements well with their first try. There need to be reflection, questioning, and feedback to clarify the desired result and to have it be one that fits the church's mission. In relation to the singles ministry illustration, the first *so that* statement for such a ministry often says, "Our church will begin a singles ministry so that singles in our church have a place to gather and share." That's a good start, but by itself it sounds as if the church is in the real estate business. Is the ultimate goal of a singles ministry to provide adequate building space for people? Such give-and-take causes people to take another step: "We want singles to have a place to gather and share *so that...*" This process can continue—using *so that* questions until together you identify the ultimate aim of the new ministry and how it grows out of and contributes to the mission of the church.

Using the two important words *so that* has the power to change the way leaders work with their congregations toward fruitfulness. *So that* can help churches think in a new way so that all that they do is shaped toward mission and results in fruitfulness.

From Fruitful Management to Fruitful Leadership: The Power of Vision

Church leaders guide their congregations to become fruitful as together they refocus their ministries directly toward the implementation of the congregation's mission. The *so that* process is one useful tool for fruitful leaders. The time, energy, effort, and commitment of everyone come together with focus and coordination so that the work of each ministry enhances the others. As we have seen, for example, the choir now selects music based not on "What do we want to sing?" but on "What will most help fulfill the worship mission?" The contributions of the choir then make it more likely that the worship mission will be fulfilled. And everything that contributes to the worship mission also makes it more likely that the church's mission becomes a reality.

These steps are at the heart of fruitful management, which is a worthy task. They provide the foundation for fruitful leadership. It is the power of vision by which fruitful management becomes fruitful leadership.

If a leader "shows up" day by day, there will always be work to do. Whether working from a *so that* model or dealing with all the things that arise in the course of a congregation's life, a leader will always find something to do. A program needs improving. Another needs expansion. There are issues among staff and volunteers that need attention. The stewardship campaign comes around, and that is a keen reminder that the current budget is not doing well. New ministry opportunities appear on the horizon.

A church leader can fill every day with worthwhile improvements, and the life of the congregation will get incrementally better. It may even get much better. But the new state of things may not represent all that fruitful leadership can be just because individual aspects of the church are working better.

THE POWER OF VISION

The essential element for fruitful church leadership is the discernment and implementation of God's vision for a community of faith at a particular time in their journey. The definition of church leadership by Scott Cormode that provided the title for Lovett's book on leading change in the church is this: Leadership is helping God's people take the next faithful step.[1]

The next faithful step is the vision to which God is calling the congregation at this point in their history and in the near future. It can be small or large. It may appear ordinary to onlookers, but to the congregation, it captures power far beyond the details of the undertaking. Fruitful *management* can be done through the dedication, good work, and persistence of pastors and lay leaders. Fruitful *leadership* is possible only through the power of God. It begins with prayerful discernment by a leader, and those with whom a leader works, around the question, "Given our mission and context, to what is God calling us now and in the near future?"

Tom describes how he came to understand vision. Years ago a church he was serving decided to build a picnic shelter.

> A church member who was a contractor stopped by and described the building to me. He talked about its size and seating capacity. He discussed how it would be situated on the property.
>
> After he heard my follow-up questions, it didn't take him long to realize that I could not envision the building that he saw so clearly in his mind. "You really can't see it, can you?" he said. Taking out a piece of paper, he sketched the shelter. Then he walked me outside and showed me exactly where it would be located. As I followed him around, he reached out as though he was touching every post. He stepped up to show the height of the concrete pad. He showed me

how tables and benches would be arranged. I stood on the empty lot as he drove off, marveling at his ability to carry a site plan and three-dimensional blueprint in his head.

Tom's brother is a landscape architect. He once donated a landscaping plan for a new parsonage that Tom's congregation was building. Looking at photos of the site and the foundation of the house that was being built, his brother drew up a plan that showed trees, shrubs, and flowers. After everything was planted, Tom called him and suggested that there had been a mistake. The shrubs were too far apart. The trees should be closer to the home. The flower beds were too wide for the small greenery that they were planting. There was silence on the other end of the line and then a question, "Tom, can't you see what this will look like in five years?"

Tom began to realize that he had never felt good at the whole "vision thing." This sometimes led him to feel inadequate when attending conferences about leading congregations. "The primary task of the leader," the speaker admonishes, "is to cast a vision for the church. It is your job to show them the Promised Land and then map the journey from here to there." The gift of leadership is often equated with the ability to envision the future of the congregation and then motivate others to share this vision. Looking around the room, Tom got the feeling that other church leaders have an organizational blueprint in their heads that he cannot see. They have a set of plans that, if followed, will lead to the health and vitality of their churches.

Over the past twenty years, the church has shown a new willingness to look to other disciplines for guidance in the area of leadership. Ideas and concepts from the business sector have been influential in changing the vocabulary and the worldview of church leaders. Much of this has been useful to the church, helping us understand practices related to leadership development, management of personnel, and financial planning and controls.

The heroes of the business world, however, tend to be men and women who have a great ability to envision the future and persuade others to join them as they move toward it. Typically, they are people whose self-confidence is in such supply that it cannot help flowing down the hallways of the corporate office building, providing the life-giving nourishment that employees need to flourish. These leaders are able to see ten or twenty years in the horizon.

Some say that Japanese business leaders use the term *long-range plan* only when they discuss the next eighty to one hundred years! How we all would like to be that kind of a leader. Church members often say that they would like to have a pastor who brings a fresh vision for the future of their church. They would like someone whose base of self-confidence is mingled with just enough humility to retain the after-taste of Christian servanthood. Some congregations desire their pastor to be a spiritual leader who assertively strides out front on the journey of faith.

The truth is that many of us have frequent periods of time when planning for the next eighty to one hundred *days* would be progress!

Lack of a clear sense of where our church will be in five years can produce a nagging sense of guilt over our vision deficiency. But the Bible gives us comfort. There we find spiritual leaders who did not have personal insight into the future so much as the ability to discern *God's* vision. Their willingness to follow that vision wherever it led made them great leaders.

Moses had no great vision on his own. His solution to the systematic oppression of the people of Israel by the most powerful government in the ancient world was to kill an Egyptian he observed beating an Israelite. The next part of his plan was to bury the man in the sand, which was guaranteed to keep ancient Egyptian CSI teams at bay for only a day or two before his problems resurfaced. Discovering that others were talking about the murder, Moses ran off to a distant land and hoped his problems would not follow him.

Esther was no visionary. Her elegance and beauty enabled her to be crowned Miss Susa in a royal beauty contest and to be chosen as the wife of King Xerxes. She concealed her Jewish ancestry from the king out of fear of repercussions. When her uncle informed her that Jews throughout the kingdom would be victims of genocide, she rose to the occasion by telling her uncle that she would rather not get involved.

Nehemiah did not start out with a vision. He was a cupbearer to King Artaxerxes, whose country had conquered Israel and destroyed the capital city. In the course of a conversation with his brother, he asked how those who remained in Jerusalem during the exile were faring. Hearing about the destruction of the city and the tentative nature of their survival, Nehemiah boldly responded by weeping. Then he prayed a prayer of confession and shared the sadness he felt with the Lord.

This type of behavior is routine for those we now view as heroic leaders from the Bible.

This is not to suggest that Moses, Esther, and Nehemiah were not leaders or did not demonstrate leadership gifts. Indeed, each came to embody God's vision for them and their people in mighty ways. Each was a part of great accomplishments for God. The key for all these leaders was to catch a glimpse of what God wanted to accomplish and then understand the role they would need to undertake if God's will was to be achieved. We are suggesting that the type of leadership found in the Bible is very different from that of a lone visionary, which we often celebrate in our culture.

GOD'S VISION IS MORE THAN THE LEADER'S VISION

Fruitful biblical leadership is about vision. It is not about a leader's vision, however, but the vision to which God is calling a people. The best leaders whom God deploys in the church and world today are not those who think up a compelling vision. They are people who can articulate God's calling for their lives and for the church. These leaders hear the calling of God and begin to follow its direction as they step into the future. The reason they often cannot describe what will happen in ten, fifteen, or twenty years is that they are carefully listening for where the Lord is trying to get them to go in their next few steps.

A central part of listening to God and looking for God's vision is asking questions. They may include the following:

- What is God trying to accomplish here?
- What can we do that would serve God's reign at this time in this place?
- How does my personal calling match what God desires?
- How can my personal gifts, graces, passion, and opportunities be put to use here?

It is from obedience to a calling from God that visions for ministry emerge. The problem with much talk of vision today is that the word *vision* is often preceded by the word *my*. Many Christians who have grown up in the culture of the United States suffer from a spirit of self-reliance that can be overcome only with a great deal of effort. It is essential for fruitful leadership that the vision we follow is not a vision we have made up on our own. Beginning with God's calling clearly shows that God is the source. It implies a discernment process that a leader does not carry out alone, something that is often missing when people describe their visions of the future. It also implies that we are servants of the Lord who calls us to particular contexts of ministry. Calling and vision together lead us to find our place in the ministry God is leading.

When we derive our vision primarily from within ourselves rather than from prayer and discernment with God's people, the problems are obvious:

- We may simply copy the efforts of others.
- The vision may be very limited compared to what God would have us do.
- Our vision may be out of alignment with God's purposes.

By contrast, when we focus on God's calling to us and seek God's vision:

- we learn that God is faithful and will provide what we need for the service we are asked to render.
- we discover that God is expansive, leading us to things that are often far beyond what we think is possible.
- we find that God knows exactly what will bring us the greatest joy, the greatest significance, and that God knows our limitations.

It is critically important for Christian leaders to understand the difference between a personal vision and God's vision. The word *vision* is used more than sixty times in the Bible. However, it is used to describe God's vision rather than someone's personal vision unrelated to God's calling. Far more frequently, more than 230 times, the phrase "the word of the Lord" occurs. When the word of the Lord comes to people in the Bible, they listen and obey to their triumph and ignore it to their peril. The word of the Lord is sometimes a whisper and sometimes a full-volume calling from God to the ear of the faithful. Either way, leadership is found in our ability to say to others, "Here is what I believe God wants us to do," and know that what we advocate is grounded in something beyond our own ideas. The best visions are never about our wishes but about God's will for our community and our servanthood of God's vision.

Fruitful Christian leadership begins the day that we are able to align the calling of God in our lives with the mission and context in which we serve. Then the vision emerges out of our community as God's people together discern the calling of God in all of our lives in light of our mission and context. It is the next faithful step toward becoming a mission-shaped church.

We know that this discernment process is neither simple nor without challenges. Church leaders and congregations have used many different tools to collect data and seek together the vision to which God is calling them at this time in their journey.[2]

Sometimes, this can be a structured and formal visioning process. At other times, a vision will emerge in surprising ways when a congregation discovers itself with a common passion for a critical need. Such was the case in the Floris Church when the congregation discovered what Tom came to call their "God-sized vision." (He shares that story in chapter 6.)

We raise two essential questions for church leaders here. To pastors, we ask, *What is the nature of your particular calling?* All pastors are called to preach, administer the sacraments, and order the life of the church. All pastors also have unique passions and interests within their general calling. One may be excited by the use of the arts in worship. Another may have deep compassion for people in economic poverty. Still another may focus on camping ministry and the ways people encounter God in the outdoors. These callings will be quite varied. It is helpful for pastors to identify these.

To other church leaders, we ask, *What brings particular joy to your congregation?* Churches have many points of commonality. Each one has its own unique identity as well. Knowing where the church experiences the most energy in ministry is helpful. It may be found in opening the church to children with special needs, or with a certain mission project, or in its desire to reach young adults in the area. When the calling and passion of pastor and the church mesh well, it is like the interconnecting of the wheels in an old clock that enables the forward momentum of the church as a whole.

Many church leaders will approach visioning in a more informal way—listening for clues as they work with church members and their wider community. Lovett is fond of reminding students who serve tiny, rural churches that they are not likely to need many surveys to learn the dreams, strengths, and needs in those congregations and communities. A discernment process is likely to happen as members talk in the parking lot after worship or gather for a potluck on Wednesday night.

A wise leader will be attentive to the culture of the congregation and approach visioning with sensitivity and respect for the people. Visioning may look different in a new congregation in comparison to well-established churches. We find challenges in both—simply different challenges. A fruitful leader must learn to navigate both the challenges and the opportunities of the leader's particular context.

CHAPTER FIVE

FRUITFUL LEADERSHIP IN ESTABLISHED CONGREGATIONS

There are challenges and opportunities in every type of congregation. Founding pastors of new congregations face hurdles that their colleagues serving established congregations do not. By the same token, founding pastors usually have considerably more immediate influence over church dynamics than other pastors do. Most pastors serve long-established congregations, and their special challenge of providing fruitful leadership is addressed in this chapter. While both of us have served several established congregations, we are going to draw from Tom's most recent experience in his current congregation.

"A GREAT OPPORTUNITY"

One of the most fruitful ministries Tom has enjoyed is the one he was least excited about entering. When his denominational supervisor asked him to become pastor of Floris United Methodist Church in 1997, the supervisor described a wonderful vision. "This is a church with a new facility that we feel can grow to have one thousand to fifteen hundred members and five hundred people in worship," he assured Tom. "You are being offered a great opportunity!"

> I drove down to look at the church facility one Saturday. It was a beautiful new building in a great location. But it also had some obvious limitations. There were about 125 parking spaces. Looking inside

the windows, I observed that the sanctuary would comfortably seat only about 150 to 200 people. I could not see how the hopes that had been shared with me could be accomplished. At the time I was serving a church I loved in a great community. I did not have much incentive to move to a new location. I called my superintendent and said that while I appreciated his offer, I thought I would decline. I explained my observation that the church was going to have parking and seating issues if it began to grow. I could not see how his goal for that church could be fulfilled.

In The United Methodist Church, pastors are appointed. In years past, clergy had little, if any, say in the process. In recent years, the appointment process has become far more collaborative among pastors, bishops, superintendents, and congregations. The opinions and situations of pastors are given far greater consideration. But it did not feel as if much had changed in 1997. The superintendent told me what an opportunity I was missing, wistfully recalled the days when pastors were servants of the church and went joyfully where they were sent, and then concluded our conversation. I called my wife and asked, "Do you like the church we are serving?"

She said that she did. "Good," I said, "because we will never be offered another appointment again!"

Everything worked out in the end. After a movement to humility and a few apologies to the superintendent, we moved to Floris United Methodist Church in Herndon, Virginia, near Washington, D.C. Here my personal calling and God's expansive vision came together. Years earlier God had given me a deep desire to see people become committed disciples of Jesus Christ. I have particular joy when people who were formerly unfamiliar with or peripherally committed to Jesus Christ find the joy of the Christian life. I also embraced the calling of God for the church to show love and compassion to the poor.

Had I remembered my calling from God and how God might have a vision for my new situation beyond my personal plans, the decision to move to this church would still have been difficult. But it would have been easy to see how God might use my particular calling in a church that had recently relocated in order to reach the community.

The most important thing you can do in your ministry is to discern what God is asking you to do with your life. The most important aspect of planning in your church is to ask what God's desire is for your congregation in its setting.

ESTABLISHED CHURCHES PRESENT UNIQUE CHALLENGES

Across the U.S. there are large teaching churches that are considered best practices congregations. When you attend their conferences, you will notice many things. The pastors and staff are usually gifted speakers who have a passion for seeing people come to faith in Jesus Christ. Cutting-edge ministries are well planned and involve large numbers of volunteers. Worship services are dynamic and well executed. Facilities are typically spacious and well designed and maintained. The combination of passion, personnel, and property can be exhilarating and leave one hopeful about what God can do in the life of a church.

It can also leave you wondering why small amounts of fruitfulness seem so difficult to cultivate in your church when such a large harvest is found elsewhere. It can leave you disheartened.

Even as we are blessed by and learn from the insights of teaching churches, we can find it a challenge to make their fruitfulness our fruitfulness. Why is it that the principles and practices of ministry they describe do not translate with greater ease? Certainly, the pastors and laypeople who come to their teaching workshops share a high commitment to Christ with those on the platform. They also have leadership gifts and good training. Yet it seems that something is hindering the application of insights from exemplary congregations into many of our churches.

It is instructive to talk with some of the church members in these teaching churches. A great deal can be discovered by spending time with people who attend a church week in and week out. The most impressive aspect of these conversations is the amazing alignment between the vision articulated by church leaders and the vision experienced by the church members in their daily lives. These people are on a mission together. They are striving for common goals. They enjoy the fact that the leaders and fellow members of their congregation share the vision that has claimed their hearts. To put it succinctly, they feel that their pastor *gets it*. The pastor feels that they *get it* as well.

One reason there is such a synergistic alignment of visions in these churches is that the founding pastor leads many teaching congregations. When not led by the founding pastor, they are often led by a pastor who arrived at a very small congregation with a compelling personal calling and an abundant preaching gift to reach the community for Christ. The rapid growth came as people were drawn to a vision they found compelling. Soon the new people represent most of the membership, and the church in many ways takes on the feel of a newly started congregation.

Here is the problem for the rest of us. Most churches, especially mainline churches, are well established, with more than one hundred years of history. This means that the pastor inherits a culture and a set of expectations that can be traced through families, pastors, and lay-persons from many generations. They have a strong sense of tradition about the *way we do things here.*

TENDING AN ORCHARD

The work of a fruitful leader in the church can be like the work of a supervisor in an apple orchard. The trees in this orchard represent the organization and ministry elements of your congregation. Which would you rather do: Be held accountable for the fruitfulness of trees you selected and planted, or inherit an orchard that has been established for years? If you choose the established orchard, there are many advantages. The work of getting things started has been done. Infrastructure is in place.

But something else is going on. This orchard has been managed by a long line of workers whose theories on tending the trees and whose goals for the orchard have changed about every decade. Over the years a variety of trees have been planted, many that cross-pollinate with bad results. Undoubtedly, there are many healthy trees in your orchard. But there are also some that are diseased and even a few that are dead. When a pastor or key leader in an established church suggests there is a need for pruning, people in the congregation may suddenly feel that a modern John the Baptist has come to town: "You brood of vipers! . . . The ax is already at the root of the trees, and every tree that does not produce good fruit will be cut down and thrown into the fire" (Luke 3:7, 9 NIV).

People may admire a prophet in their Bible. They rarely enjoy listening to one in their sanctuary. For most of us, the deep rooting of the past is the reason that the present and future can be so difficult.

There is good news. Long before the current generation of leaders took charge at your church, God was calling it to fruitfulness. God had a vision for your church from the beginning, and God has a vision for your church today. It is a vision of health, vitality, relevance, and service. God is calling you and your congregation to see this vision. Again, the important thing to remember here is that you are being called to fulfill God's vision. The key is to discover the story of God's calling for the congregation.

LEARN THE STORY

An essential prerequisite for fruitful leadership in established churches is to learn the story of the congregation. God's vision will emerge partly out of that history, and you must be in a position to tie a new vision to past visions of the congregation. You will draw from the historical story even as you are discovering and telling the story of God's new vision for the church.

The key to discovering the vision to which God is calling your congregation is to learn the story of the church. Whether we like it or not, the past in an established church has tremendous impact on the present and the future. Like an archaeologist, you have to discover it. Like a social scientist, you have to analyze it. Like a theologian, you have to interpret it. Like a politician, you have to manage it. The Christ-honoring portions of your church's history are sacred not only to the people but also to God. It is the story of God's mighty acts in history through this particular community of faith.

People who have been in a church a long time love to talk about the life they have enjoyed there. They feel complimented when you ask them how the church has changed over time and what values have remained the same. If you will spend time with longtime members learning the history of the church, they will spread the word that you are interested in the life of that congregation. This is important because their greatest fear is the pastor who brings a big agenda that he or she is going to place on the church regardless of the church's needs or desires.

When you spend time discovering the history, values, and story of the church, you send a message that you are trying to join them on the journey that God has been leading over many decades. Unlike the pastor of a new church, you are not the original leader. You are one of many who have already served and one of many who will lead in the future. Honor the long line of clergy and laity who have gone before you and who have faithfully pursued God's calling. Find ways to affirm them at every turn. Build your credibility by honoring the calling of God that the church has fulfilled in the past.

The key to your future together is found in the intersection of the unique calling of the pastor and the vision of God that has claimed the attention of the congregation.

KNOW THE GARDEN YOU ARE TENDING

Church leadership is a lot like gardening. Gardeners have to know their particular spot of earth well enough to know what can grow and what cannot. Since moving to Kansas City, I learned through trial and much error which plants grow in the crazy Midwest weather and impermeable clay soil.

The same is true of our leadership in congregations. No two congregations are the same. We cannot count on our favorite tricks to work in every situation. Each person, group, and situation is unique and calls for spiritually discerning creativity. Because God is present and active in every context in a unique way, we need to adjust to the special ways that the Holy Spirit is working. To serve faithfully, we need to get to know our contexts of ministry up close and on the inside, so that we come to see the situation *as God sees it*. To see with God's eyes is the bedrock of leadership in the church.

Just as right bulbs need to be planted at the right time in the right soil, leaders need to discern God's vision and plan far ahead for spiritual harvest. Cultivating our gardens and our congregations requires visionary and deliberate planning.[1]
Robert K. Martin

LEARNING LEVERAGE POINTS FOR THE FUTURE

In any church there are some members living in God's past and others longing for God's future. Everyone else falls in between. Often those with the greatest attachment to the past are like large boulders in a river around which every decision affecting the church's future must flow. If a growing current of change unites too many of these boulders, they can form a virtual dam that will completely obstruct leaders in the congregation from making important decisions or taking actions that lead the church into the future.

The good news is that the congregation's own story and values can often act as a lever that has the power to encourage these members to move toward the future. They typically honor the history of their congregation highly. They want see the church live consistently with its heritage. The beauty of the congregation's story is that it allows the leaders to remind the congregation of the very best of its history and how these qualities can still be lived in the community today. New members also benefit from the story. It acts as a portal through which they step into community. As all learn the story, the church becomes a part of everyone who shares its values, celebrates its past, and is called to the future.

Listening to people talk about Floris United Methodist Church, Tom kept hearing a number of recurring themes:

- Make Christ the center of our lives. Floris was a church that desired to bring Christ to the center of people's lives. The decision to leave a small facility with more than one hundred years of history had been a painful one, but at its core was a desire to help new residents to the community build a relationship with Jesus Christ.
- Continue to make it a church at the center of the community. Floris had always been at the center of its community. For years all sorts of community events were held at Floris.
- Be willing to widen the circle. Floris had always been a church that helped newcomers assimilate into the community. One couple, retired and whose children were now grown and had families of their own, could still recount the first time they visited the congregation as a young family. The warm welcome and follow-up invitations had made their family feel at home in their new community.
- Care for others. Floris cared about people's needs and felt the call of God to assist the lonely, the poor, and those who had no one to care for them in the community.
- Serve Christ. Church members used their gifts and talents to serve God and, in the process, matured as Christians.

After the themes were identified, they needed to be tested. Members with the longest tenure were asked whether they were true. Was it accurate to say that Floris was a church that wanted Christ to be the center of a person's life? Was it true to say that in years past, Floris had been a center of its community or that it had a value of caring for people who were economically poor or who had special needs? Not only did the members who best knew the church confirm the themes; they added new stories to illustrate them. They shared accounts of past church members who lived out the highest values of the congregation. One could sense their energy building as they recalled the ways the church had served Christ in the past and imagined that their church could serve Christ just as faithfully in the future.

These themes are critical to the vision to which God is calling the congregation. Values from the past are essential to fuel energy for the future. There must be an alignment between where God is calling the church to go and at least some of its cherished values. Fruitful ministry begins when the congregation and pastor are together on achieving God's vision in ways consistent with the best of the church's heritage.

As these themes and stories were shared, more members came forward with new stories about ways in which they had experienced these values. As people talked about these principles of past ministry, it became obvious that they were beginning to resonate with newer members. It became more comfortable to share this emerging interpretation of the church's story with the congregation during sermons, new member classes, and newsletter articles. It became the foundation from which God's calling for the future could be discerned.

During a long-range planning session, the group spent time studying the Book of Acts and talking about the church's past. People discussed times in their history when Floris had experienced *signs and wonders* that are associated with the presence of the Holy Spirit. At the time of the planning session, the church was in its sixth year in a new facility but already beginning to outgrow it. Sometime during that day, it was suggested that if the church were going to remain at the center of its growing community, it would have to relocate and build a third facility on a larger parcel of land that could accommodate parking and seating for those visiting the church.

Tom was hearing the calling of God to take such a leap of faith, but he knew what a difficult decision that would be for so many who had sacrificed to move to the current facility. One of the senior members of that committee, who was a lifelong member of the church, spoke: "I would like to put a big sign in front of the building that reads, 'We are full. There are lots of nice churches around here with plenty of seating. Go there.' But when I think about our Bible study and how our church has always been open to new people in our community, I think we have no choice but to consider relocating again. Just don't ask me to be on this building committee!"

That one statement saved the church hours of discussion and debate about relocation. It was in itself a sign and a wonder. This is the power of understanding God's past calling to a congregation. Everything you need for the ministry in front of you is typically already behind you. You must discern it, agree on it, and begin to articulate it in the church.

YOUR CHURCH'S CREATION STORY

In his book *The Contrarian's Guide to Leadership*, University of Southern California president Steven Sample makes the case that an important task for all leaders is to discern the *creation story* for the organizations they lead.[2] The creation story is a brief overview of the organization's history. It includes how the organization got started, what motivated its founders, notable accomplishments over the years, and why it is important today. It should be an engaging story that lasts no more than about five minutes. This story should

- be true,
- appeal to church members as a story that honors their past,
- appeal to those who the leader hopes will become part of the church,
- emphasize that the church has changed over time while remaining true to core values, and
- engender pride in the past that makes hope in the future a foregone conclusion.

Congregational creation stories have a biblical precedent. The Lord commanded the people of Israel to recite such a story when they took their offering to the priest in the Promised Land:

> Then you shall declare before the LORD your God: "My father was a wandering Aramean, and he went down into Egypt with a few people and lived there and became a great nation, powerful and numerous.

But the Egyptians mistreated us and made us suffer, putting us to hard labor. Then we cried out to the LORD, the God of our fathers, and the LORD heard our voice and saw our misery, toil and oppression. So the LORD brought us out of Egypt with a mighty hand and an outstretched arm, with great terror and with miraculous signs and wonders. He brought us to this place and gave us this land, a land flowing with milk and honey; and now I bring the firstfruits of the soil that you, O LORD, have given me." (Deuteronomy 26:5-10 NIV)

This brief history was used to remind future generations of the humble beginnings of their ancestors, the way God sustained them during hard times, and described the present in a way that led people to feel hope for their future.

When you are making choices about what to include in the creation story of your church, you have the opportunity to talk about the elements of its calling and journey that are consistent with your calling today. It should be honest. It may mention things in the church that did not go well and hard times through which members felt God's sustaining power. It should also include what was learned and what values emerged that now shape the congregation in positive ways.

The strength of the creation story in the established church is that it allows you to gain consensus regarding the broad vision that God has held for your church in the past and present as well as the calling you are hearing for the future. As you share this story from the pulpit, in new member classes, and in the community, a new consensus can emerge regarding the ministry and values of this congregation.

CREATION STORY FOR FLORIS UNITED METHODIST CHURCH

Floris Church was established over one hundred years ago by a small group of people who wanted to enjoy the benefits of American Methodism, with its emphasis on personal holiness, social outreach, and dynamic worship. The founders first met for Sunday school and then worship services led monthly by a Methodist preacher or a layperson. The first facility was built in 1895 out of a desire for Christ to be at the center of their lives and the church to be at the center of the community. Over the years Floris proved itself a church where people were willing to widen the circle for those who wanted a community in which to worship and live. New residents were invited to become part of the church with neighbors and friends. The church became a center of community functions for school graduations, weddings, funerals, and cooperative ministries among congregations. Members over the decades reached out to others to offer ministries that blessed the lives of local residents, displayed compassion to those in need, and met needs of the community.

In the 1980s, when the Herndon community rapidly expanded, members made a difficult decision to leave behind their historic church building, purchase new land, and construct a modern facility. A smaller church that enjoyed tight-knit relationships knew it would please God to widen its circle for new residents. Within five years it became evident that the new location was too small if Floris UMC was to continue to welcome its growing community. Another difficult decision was made to purchase a new property and build a larger facility so that the circle could widen again. During this period, outreach to those struggling with poverty and other needs extended farther into the community and world than ever before, offering members ever-growing opportunities to serve Christ by serving others.

Understanding the story was essential to leading the congregation and the discernment of God's next steps for the congregation.

FROM MISSION TO VISION

In the years since then, the church has far exceeded anything that Tom might have hoped at the beginning. The mission of Floris's denomination is "to make disciples of Jesus Christ for the transformation of the world." Sometimes denominational missions do not fit particular congregations. But Floris did see its mission as both reaching people for Christ and redeeming the world. The mission shaped every ministry of the church.

Through wonderful lay and staff leadership, growing numbers of members, generous stewardship, and much hard work, the congregation made great progress in living out the mission in better and more expansive ways. Over a period of ten years, the church grew from a worship attendance of three hundred to an attendance of one thousand persons each Sunday. Worship expanded from two to five services with a variety of musical styles and one service in Spanish that reaches out to an immigrant community. In 2006 the congregation relocated to a new facility that has space for additional seating and parking for future

53

growth. The outreach ministry to the community and world is beyond anything it has ever done in the past.

"What a shame if my limited vision had stifled God's calling" is Tom's reflection on his experience at Floris.

As well as Floris was doing by "everyone doing their jobs well" and showing growth in every aspect of ministry, God still had a vision for the congregation far beyond incremental improvement of existing ministries.

CHAPTER SIX

SERVING GOD'S VISION: ONE PASTOR'S STORY

By most standards, the leadership that Tom had provided at Floris United Methodist Church appeared effective and even fruitful. Floris had a clear mission. Its values were rooted in Christian faith and years of faithful ministry. Programs were well managed, and the church was growing. But Tom discovered he had never truly understood fruitful leadership until he and the congregation opened themselves not only to God's vision but also to what he came to call a "God-sized vision."

GOD-SIZED VISIONS

Sitting in churches every Sunday are people looking for significance. Like Simeon and Anna in the Temple, they have been waiting and hoping for a long time that their lives would be given to something meaningful. Many have lost hope that they will find the fulfillment of this search. They are aware that their lives are full of the mundane. They need to buy groceries and coordinate carpools; they need to change the oil and meet deadlines. The older people get, the more of life there is to manage. There is maintenance to perform on everything from houses to relationships. Soon the dreams of the past and the goals we hoped to achieve begin to languish under the hot sun of daily existence. Anxiety about the future exacerbates the problem. Questions about paying for children's education or retirement or just meeting current obligations suck the creative energy that might have been applied to consideration of how my life could be used to have an impact on the needs of the world.

Deep inside most of us is the thought: *There must be more than this.* Yet most people are aware that given all the plates they have spinning, they will never be able to do the fulfilling things they once envisioned.

It may be that one of the central reasons that Christ calls his followers to live in community is to enable them to fulfill their lifelong quest for significance. God knows our limitations sooner and in greater detail than we do. God knows that most of us will never accomplish the greatest dreams of our hearts alone, but that we would find great joy in joining others on such a pursuit. Christ called his disciples to live as though something was at stake in their efforts to advance the reign of God.

In 1999, the Reverend John Yambasu, a pastor from Sierra Leone, Africa, preached at Floris and told the congregation about the suffering that people in his country had endured during their decade-long civil war. Sierra Leone had been at or near the bottom of international lists of poor countries for several years prior to the outbreak of war. The destruction of villages, schools, hospitals, churches, roads, and municipal centers during the war assured that it would remain there for years to come. God used John's words to touch the hearts of the people sitting in the pews that Sunday. Weeks, even months later, members of the church were asking how Floris was going to answer his call to relieve the suffering of our brothers and sisters in Christ in Sierra Leone.

When we asked John for some direction regarding our response, he suggested that we focus our attention on children in the interior of the country. Children had been dramatically affected by the war. Many had parents killed during the fighting and did not even have distant family members to care for them. The fact that the family network was so strained by war and poverty that some children were left without caregivers was unthinkable to the citizens of Sierra Leone, and yet real. Orphaned children needed the care of the church. Such a ministry would have to be ongoing. We would need to think in terms of years rather than months, but it would bless children, the most vulnerable population.

THE POWER OF A GOD-SIZED VISION

John had helped the Floris congregation understand that something was at stake and that we had both the possibility and the responsibility to respond. We also understood that we had never undertaken anything like this in the history of our church. That brought great excitement and great trepidation to our leaders.

What started as a loosely defined desire to help children in Africa was to become the vision that God revealed to our congregation. The congregation did not need a carefully designed visioning process to discern this vision. They already had a firm grasp of their mission, values, and story: *serving Christ, caring for others, widening the circle.* Once they were confronted by the unspeakable tragedy of Sierra Leone's children, the vision grew quickly. They also thought they had or could find resources—though none of us had any idea at the time what that would mean.

There is nothing more exciting in the church than to know that something is at stake and that the church is courageous enough to respond. God-sized visions are an essential part of fruitful leadership because they give people an opportunity to experience the significance of answering God's calling. They give people the passion to accomplish what they are called to do.

The problem in many churches related to fruitfulness is not that so much is at stake but that priorities are underresourced. "We would do more if we had more," we like to say of ourselves. The problem is that so little is at stake that there is nothing to which church members can dedicate themselves. "We would do more if we had something to do," may be what the people of the congregation are saying if we just listened.

The resulting spiritual anemia is the reason that many churches are so vulnerable to the diseases of dissension, division, and strife. When there is little at stake in a church's ministry, the vacuum will call out the worst side of members. Rather than work to share Christ or alleviate the suffering of those in need, members fill idle time with bad habits like gossip and criticism that are destructive to the body of Christ. When a congregation strives after God-sized visions, it has little time and energy for petty bickering or people with a critical spirit. In the face of important work to be accomplished, such people simply look small.

Fruitful ministry requires leaders to embrace God-sized visions that have the power to transform the lives, church, and community of their people. A God-sized vision is something that your church cannot do under its own power with the resources available today. It is large enough to cause even faithful church members to ask, "Have you lost your mind?"

BEGINNING A GOD-SIZED VISION

It is essential that God-sized visions flow from the calling experienced by the leader and the church. Such visions must be carefully discerned and humbly received and not simply become the bluster of leaders looking for a new rush of organizational adrenaline to get things revved up around the church. The reason that this is so important is that a God-sized vision requires the Lord's ongoing blessing to be accomplished. It is the application of the old encouragement for the church to do what God is blessing rather than asking God to bless what you are doing.

In December 1999, nations around the world were preparing to celebrate the coming of the year 2000. Floris used this opportunity to invite gifts to a Millennial Offering to celebrate two thousand years of the presence of Jesus Christ. Members of the congregation were challenged to consider how they would respond when their grandchildren asked what they did to celebrate this historic occasion. "Will you tell them about a party you attended or a cruise you took?" members were asked. "None of these things will mean anything to you in forty years. Why not tell them that you were part of a church that went to one of the poorest countries in the world to help children, the most vulnerable population, and did something beautiful for God?"

Tom recalls the goal was $25,000 to start a ministry to orphaned children called the Child Rescue Centre. This name was given to us by our partners in the United Methodist Church in Sierra Leone. Under the direction of Bishop Joseph Humper, we shared a calling and a vision of caring for children who had no place to turn except the church. We put a thermometer in the entry of the church displaying our $25,000 goal. By the end of the first week in December, contributions overran the top of the thermometer. We created a new one for week two with a goal of $50,000. It was surpassed by the end of the week. By the end of December, the Millennial Offering had received more than $125,000. Our God-sized vision had inspired a new level of sacrificial giving for children we had never met in a land we had never visited. Floris welcomed the year 2000 with joy and excitement that were palpable among the members.

God-sized visions may sound similar to big, audacious goals advocated by secular writers. But there is one big difference. God-sized visions can be accomplished only with the power of the Holy Spirit. When they are fulfilled, the church responds not with congratulatory praise of its organizational ability or depth of commitment, even though these are necessary. These visions are so large that the church can only stand back and wonder at the way God's power has been present in their midst. The fulfillment of a God-sized vision is deeply spiritual because it leads people to experience humility and gratitude before God rather than the sin of pride.

When we embrace God's vision, the presence of the Holy Spirit is easily discerned in the life of the church. Such an experience is essential to the vitality of the congregation. It is the moment when Simeon and Anna realize that something very special is about to happen in the Lord's Temple. The Bible often refers to God's willingness to accomplish *signs and wonders* to assist the people of God in their efforts toward God's reign. Moses warns Pharaoh not to get in the way of the Lord, who will use signs and wonders to clear obstacles from the path of God's people. The term is found in words of the prophets, who remind Israel of the signs and wonders of the past and who testify to God's use of them in the present.

Luke uses this term from the Old Testament to show the continuity of God's work in the lives of Christ's followers. In Acts 14, Paul and Barnabas speak with great power at a synagogue in Iconium. When people begin to respond to their message by believing in Jesus Christ, the officials of the synagogue are angered and work to turn the crowd against the apostles. Even so, the work of the Spirit could not be impeded. Luke writes, "So Paul and Barnabas spent considerable time there, speaking boldly for the Lord, who confirmed the message of his grace by enabling them to do miraculous signs and wonders" (v. 3 NIV).

The reason God-sized visions are so captivating is that they literally come to fill every thought and conversation. They give buoyancy to everyone. You feel good just being associated with such an endeavor. There is joy in its service. But in the midst of all the fun and excitement, a strange transformation can take place. The vision that has been such a source of energy turns into something frightening. Confident plans for the future suddenly turn into questions about the reality of what we have begun. People say, "What have we gotten ourselves into?"

Make no mistake. God-sized visions lead to human anxieties:

- Can I control it?
- Can I contain it?
- How will I ever nourish it enough?
- What is going to happen if it really is turned loose?

Suddenly, a romp through a field becomes a struggle to keep a monster at bay. The leader will begin to have inner doubts that he or she may not be willing to raise with others for fear of dispiriting the team. Yet the questions grow louder in one's head:

- Can I really handle it?
- Am I the right leader for this?
- What if people discover that I am not sure what I am doing?

This is the problem with God's visions: they are God-sized! If they were easily accomplished, someone would already have accomplished them. When you add the physical and spiritual exhaustion that often accompany them, leaders will begin to feel overwhelmed.

MAINTAINING THE VISION

Tom discovered it does not take long to spend $125,000. This was a surprise. It was, after all, the largest special offering ever taken at our church. It is a large sum of money. But it does not take long to spend it when you are renovating a building; feeding, clothing, and educating forty children in residence; and supporting others in the community.

A small team from Floris went to Bo, Sierra Leone, to see the Child Rescue Centre (CRC) in January 2002. We landed the day after the formal declaration of peace in the country. Our team included two doctors, a nurse, and three willing servants. Our primary task was to see how the work of our partners in Sierra Leone was progressing and to assess the health of the children and staff of the CRC. We spent time getting to know the children and staff, solidifying our partnership with them, and allaying fears that we would be there today and gone tomorrow, like so many disappointing efforts in Africa.

The team returned to Floris with a positive report of the ministry that was developing in Sierra Leone. The CRC was a blessing to forty children who lived there and more than one hundred children whose education and medical care were supported in the community. It was a blessing to be a part of something that made a difference.

Two months later the church business manager reported that funds for CRC would be depleted shortly. Were we into something over our heads? It felt that way. It is an understatement to say this predicament caused high anxiety. It also led to sleepless nights, which provided great opportunities to seek God in prayer. As the faces of the forty children filled my mind, I knew there would be a solution if we sought it from God.

A cursory reading of the Bible reveals that God is comfortable with our feeling overwhelmed. God routinely calls us to things that we cannot accomplish on our own, perhaps so we will seek community with the Holy Spirit and fellow believers.

LESSONS ABOUT GOD-SIZED VISIONS FROM ZERUBBABEL

One great account of a God-sized vision in the Scripture begins in the ruined Jerusalem of 538 B.C. Almost fifty years after its destruction, the capital city was a mere glimpse of its former glory during the reign of King Solomon. In 586 B.C., the Babylonian army successfully assaulted its walls, overran its defenses, and took control of the capital city of Judah. The Babylonians' desire was to leave the people of Jerusalem with no hope. They burned homes, toppled the city walls in most locations, and brought destruction everywhere. Finally, in an act that probably had more to do with theology than the tactics of war, they looted the treasure from the Temple, which was the epicenter of Jewish worship, and then destroyed the structure. The leading citizens of Jerusalem were rounded up and forced to march to Babylon, where they would live in exile. It is not difficult to imagine the grief they would have felt walking past the ruined Temple. It signified the defeat of Yahweh at the hands of Marduk, the god of the Babylonians.

The prophets of Judah shared a different grief. The destruction of Jerusalem and the Temple was not about the power of God but about the lack of faithfulness among the people. The people of Judah had turned away from God in every way, from the worship of idols to the mistreatment of the poor. Over time they had become as broken as the stones that were once the walls of the great Temple but that now lay in the street.

Sometime around 538 B.C., King Cyrus issued an edict that gave permission for Jews exiled in Babylon to return to Jerusalem. During this time, Zerubbabel heard a calling from God that can only be described

61

as a God-sized vision: *rebuild the Temple in Jerusalem*. One can imagine the joy it brought to Zerubbabel to know that the God of Israel had not forgotten such a disobedient and ungrateful people.

1. Understand Why the Vision Is Significant

Zerubbabel seems to understand that his calling is not simply to rebuild the Temple of God. It is to rebuild the people of God by restoring their spiritual life. The great leaders who restored Jerusalem and the nation of Israel at this time seemed to understand the principle of *so that*. Nehemiah understood that the city walls would have to be rebuilt *so that* the people could be secure. Ezra understood that the Law would have to be read *so that* people could be obedient. Zerubbabel understood that the Temple would have to be rebuilt *so that* people could renew their relationship with God in worship. All of these leaders were working to restore the ancient vision of the relationship between a holy people and a holy God.

Zerubbabel must have felt that he had things in hand. It was as if he were out to walk his friendly puppy as he journeyed with other exiles that King Cyrus of Persia had allowed to return to Jerusalem.

2. There Is a Reason God Does Not Show You Everything

As is often the case in the life of leaders, it was not long before that puppy turned into something out of control. Zerubbabel had to manage problems and conflicts he probably never imagined were possible when working for the Creator of the Universe.

His God-sized vision met mixed reviews. When the foundation for the new Temple was laid out, the crowd was divided. Some wept with joy to think that proper worship would be reestablished in Jerusalem. But many older people wept with grief when they saw that the size of the new Temple would in no way approach the glory of the Temple that King Solomon had constructed. For these people the new Temple was another reminder that Jerusalem would never be fully restored.

If it was not enough to have such mixed reviews from the people of Jerusalem, soon the leaders of the Samaritans joined to block the construction of the Temple. They raised fears that a rebellion could be on the way, and the work of the Temple was impeded for eighteen years.

Zerubbabel had to become a project administrator during this time as memoranda went back and forth among the governor of the Trans-

Euphrates, the king of Persia, and the local officials in Jerusalem. Old records had to be located. The workers had to be encouraged and kept on task as rival officials worked to shut down the project.

What is absent in the Book of Ezra or in the words of the prophets who mention Zerubbabel is any indication that God warned him of the hardships and hassles that he would face. The reason that God does not show us the difficulty of the journey to our destination is that if we could see it, we would never begin. God is content to let us experience the joy of a significant calling that motivates us to move forward so that we will simply get started.

One of the important issues to understand about God-sized visions is that many wise and discerning people do not undertake them because they can see the problems they will create. God-sized visions require people with a certain level of trust in the Lord that could easily be described as foolishness. The apostle Paul put it this way in 1 Corinthians 1:26-29:

> Brothers, think of what you were when you were called. Not many of you were wise by human standards; not many were influential; not many were of noble birth. But God chose the foolish things of the world to shame the wise; God chose the weak things of the world to shame the strong. He chose the lowly things of this world and the despised things—and the things that are not—to nullify the things that are, so that no one may boast before him. (NIV)

Our task is not to have the entire plan mapped out but to take the next faithful step that God is calling us to take regarding the completion of the vision.

3. God-sized Visions Give God Room to Work

A very instructive passage is found in Ezra 5:5: "The eye of their God was watching over the elders of the Jews, and they were not stopped until a report could go to Darius and his written reply be received" (NIV).

When we discern the vision God has for us, signs and wonders of God will begin to display themselves in ways we never imagined possible. Not only did the work miraculously continue, but Darius, king of Persia, sent word that the Temple was to be completed and he would provide all the materials. Anyone who attempted to stop it would be put to death. The exiles were able to celebrate the first Passover that the people of Israel had enjoyed in Jerusalem in a generation. The scene in Ezra 6:21-22 describes both the joy of the people and the wonder they felt for the miracles God had displayed:

> The Israelites who had returned from the exile ate [the Passover meal], together with all who had separated themselves from the unclean practices of their Gentile neighbors in order to seek the LORD, the God of Israel. For seven days they celebrated with joy the Feast of Unleavened Bread, because the LORD had filled them with joy by changing the attitude of the king of Assyria, so that he assisted them in the work on the house of God, the God of Israel. (NIV)

Zerubbabel began to understand that this vision was not all on his shoulders. He was simply a servant for the Lord who was more than willing to perform *signs and wonders* that no one could explain so that the Temple could be restored. Looking back on this experience, Zerubbabel and those who worked on the Temple were obviously amazed at the king's generous provision of permission and materials to build the Temple. God has a way of exceeding our wildest expectations if we will give the Spirit room to work.

Exceeding of expectations has not stopped. God did something amazing when the Child Rescue Centre was about to run out of funds. The Spirit of God raised up the most unlikely group that I could imagine in our church: golfers. After we shared our funding dilemma with key leaders in the congregation, one man offered to put together a team to host a golf tournament. Soon the idea gained momentum as people volunteered to lead this effort. Many in this group were men whose church attendance was especially sporadic in the summer because they were on the golf course. A new enthusiasm began to grow in their group as they realized they could use their favorite sport to feed children in Sierra Leone. The first CRC golf tournament raised enough money to cover six months of operating expenses for the CRC and created a team of people who had such fun together that they promised to make it an annual event.

The other calling that God used to sustain the CRC was through the wider community. Many of us began to realize that our church was a more vital and faith-filled congregation as a result of the CRC. The blessing of this ministry seemed to be overflowing into every other area. Local outreach to the community increased. Stewardship was more faithful. As people traveled to the CRC on short-term mission trips, they brought the joy and energy of the African church back with them.

It occurred to us that rather than contact other churches to ask for a few dollars to assist orphaned children, we should invite them to experience the vitality and joy of a God-sized vision. Visiting other churches, we told them about the way the CRC was blessing our congregation and asked if they would like to become partners with us in what God was doing through the church in Sierra Leone. Today the CRC partnership includes twelve congregations that have made a commitment to give a minimum of $5,000 per year for five years. These congregations send mission teams to lend a hand at the CRC. Many give far more than the $5,000 minimum. Through this partnership, we have had the opportunity to get to know the CRC children and staff and one another. We have found community in the vision we are attempting to fulfill. As a result, the CRC has been able to expand greatly the number of children it serves in the community and in residence. It now touches more than 250 children through the residential, foster care, and support-a-child programs. The first generation of CRC-related kids are attending vocational schools or college to prepare for adult life. After a new facility for the children was constructed, the building they once occupied was turned into a hospital. Mercy Hospital, led by a Sierra Leonean doctor and staff, now sees more than eight hundred patients a month and offers hope to those who have no other access to medical care.

4. Growing the Leader

One result of engaging in God-sized visions is the impact they can have on the spiritual life of the leader. Imagine someone coming to Zerubbabel for advice a few years after the Temple was built. This person is having a crisis of faith and has an important decision to make that will impact the family. This person wants to be faithful to God but fears the ramifications of such fidelity. In such moments, the leader must be absolutely convinced that God can be trusted to care for us if we will choose to be obedient. Zerubbabel may not have walked this person through the Temple and told his story, but his confidence in God's provision would have been a sufficient testimony of his experience.

God-sized visions will challenge and stretch the leader more than any other aspect of ministry. They are challenging because they move us off the status quo. The chaos of this daunting vision will seem to have the upper hand many days and leave us wondering how we ever could have been convinced to begin. When we remain faithful, however, the provision and grace of the Holy Spirit often bring a surprising conclusion to God-sized visions. Things get better. The memory of the hardest moments remains with us, but the joy of their company and the sense of significance to which they have led us make it all worthwhile.

In the process of our working to accomplish great things with God, the Holy Spirit has a way of teaching us the most important lessons of our faith. We learn that God loves us and God is faithful. We learn that God longs for us to join in the work of advancing God's reign so that Christ will be exalted, the good news will be preached to the poor, and people looking for significance will be able to tell stories to their grandchildren about the signs and wonders that God did in their midst.

CHAPTER SEVEN

GIVING LIFE TO THE VISION

William is the chair of the outreach committee at his church. Upon returning from a mission trip to Guatemala, he was anxious to talk about the experience with his church family so that they could also share such a life-changing event. Building stoves for fellow Christians who live in the rain forest introduced William to a new culture and the deep faith of those who live in subsistence-level poverty and trust Christ in ways that William never imagined. On the return flight, he anticipated the impact of an ongoing relationship between members of his church and the villages where he worked. He was certain that this relationship would bring vitality to his church while improving community health in Guatemala.

The energy William felt his first Sunday home soon faded. He shared his story with his pastor and other leaders in the church. He spoke to friends and even a few groups in the congregation. Yet nothing happened as a result. The idea never gained momentum. Plans were never made. Support was not found. William soon was discouraged about his role as a leader and about his church as well.

Those who desire fruitful ministry should not underestimate the difficulty of building the necessary consensus to make great ideas a reality. One of the greatest gifts that church leaders can provide for one another and members of their congregation is clarity around the calling of God they share. (We previously noted this characteristic among teaching churches.) Clarity about the mission and vision acts as a magnetic force that pulls people together. When such clarity is present, it supplies a vitality that naturally occurs when people discover that they are on a mission together. When clarity is absent, every good idea presented by members of the church is of equal merit and produces equal frustration when neglected.

Clarity about mission and vision enables the congregation to understand why decisions are made. The problem in most churches is not that there are good ideas competing with bad ideas for scarce resources. Rather, there are good ideas competing with other good ideas. Clarity around God's calling upon the church enables members of the congregation to work in harmony with one another. Clarity draws out good ideas that serve the congregation's vision so that they can become real ministries. Clarity also gently pushes out ideas that may have merit but do not serve the larger vision of the congregation.

It is true that sermons and board meetings and church dinners can lack meaning and focus without a clear shared vision. It is also true that a shared vision, even a God-sized vision, is unlikely to come to life if a congregation lacks structures and processes through which they communicate and carry out such a vision. The vision becomes a lens through which a congregation sees every part of its ministry. And every congregation must discover and create the avenues through which its vision comes to fruition.

Each congregation has its own culture, its own sense of *how we do things around here*. There are usually formal structures in each place, but sometimes through the informal structures a vision emerges and is enlivened. In some small churches, for example, the parking lot conversations are the locus of decision making. In other churches, the Wednesday night Bible study is the place where intimations of a new vision will emerge. Some will say that, in their congregation, nothing will happen unless the women's mission study group catches the vision.

Leaders who seek to be fruitful leaders will learn the culture of their church and community. Thus they will learn how to help a congregation discover its shared vision and bring it to life. The structures and processes will differ. But a vision not embodied through some kinds of structures and processes, however informal, is unlikely to bear fruit. Building a clear and solid set of structures allows churches to continue growing to be vibrant, faithful, and joy-filled churches.

In the large church where Tom serves, leaders have developed numerous processes that have proved to be valuable for the health and fruitfulness of the congregation. This church has spent a great deal of time investing in physical structures to advance the mission of the congregation. Leaders realized they needed to make a similar investment in organizational structures that would enable future ministry. These might take different forms in other places, but they suggest a series of tasks that all congregations would do well to take into account if they yearn for their visions to be fruitful.

MAKING A VISION LIVE AT FLORIS CHURCH

Three groups must share clarity around the vision: the governing board, the church staff, and the members of the congregation. There are methods to use with each group to ensure clear communication regarding the intentions of the church and its ministry. This communication is critical to giving life to the vision.

The Governing Board

The governing board of the church must have a common understanding of the focus of the church's vision at any given time. It is also important that this group share a common statement of initiatives for the coming year that will give shape to the vision. One significant result of this clarity is that it builds the relationship between the laity and their pastor. By updating annually the key church initiatives, the pastor and governing board will remain in step with each other. If this process is neglected, the competition of good ideas raised by the pastor, leaders, and church members may soon turn divisive. Such clarity is essential if the efforts of pastors and governing boards are to attain outcomes rather than simply talk about outcomes; that is, if they are to become fruitful congregations.

A tool that can assist in this effort is a monthly monitoring report of a church initiative. If a church has five key initiatives for the coming year, the governing board should hear a report about progress on one to two of them each month. A progress report is a written document presented by the pastor, staff person, or key volunteer leader that reflects the plans of leaders related to this initiative. The report will include the following:

- A statement of desired outcome
- Interpretation of the statement, including intermediate goals that address the outcome statement

- Success indicators that describe the nature of the fruit that each goal will produce
- Action plans that describe what will happen to meet each goal listed

Some may feel that such a suggestion is somehow too businesslike for the church. But imagine for a moment how such an ongoing conversation among members of the governing board of the church could serve the desire for fruitfulness in ministry as well as enhance the relationships among key leaders in the church who desire the guidance of the Holy Spirit in their deliberations. Consider how much more support the board could offer the pastor, staff, and other leaders if there was a common understanding of key initiatives for living out the vision. And consider how much more the board could engage with those initiatives. Here are some possible relational benefits that would occur:

- Pastor and staff time: The board could interpret to church members how the pastor and staff spend time and how such time allocations serve the ministry.
- Authority issues: Consensus forged during monthly meetings around ministry initiatives protects the pastor and staff from being seen as autocratic or working on personal agendas.
- Spiritual gifts: Clarity around goals and assignment of leadership encourages good use of everyone's gifts and abilities to focus in areas that she or he will pursue with greatest success.
- Role clarity: Key leaders are on the same page and avoid role conflict and confusion.
- Leadership discernment: The dialogue enables the church and the pastor to understand whether they have a good match regarding the interests, desires, and calling of the church and the calling of the pastor rather than dealing with such important questions through conflict and crisis.
- Unity in the body of Christ: Monitoring reports enable the church leaders to be engaged in the initiatives of the church so that they can build consensus among the church as a whole. They enable strong teamwork among the staff, the governing board, and members of the congregation.

- Spiritual conversation: By revisiting key initiatives in formal conversation over the course of a year, the governing board and pastoral leaders take time at several points to discern the work of the Holy Spirit in their midst. Goals and plans can then be adjusted for greater faithfulness and fruitfulness.

The Church Staff

A second key group that must have clarity around the vision and key initiatives embraced by the congregation is the church staff. No group of people has the ability to think of more good ideas that compete for limited human and financial resources in a congregation than the people who work there each day. They see the impact of the church's ministry and have multiple conversations with key leaders and church members each week. They are also experts in their fields of ministry and feel deep passion for their particular areas of service.

For these reasons, the church staff must have clarity around the broader ministry of the church they serve so that they avoid the conflicts described by Paul in 1 Corinthians 12. In this well-known passage, Paul imagines a body whose parts are in conflict with one another because they have forgotten the interconnected nature of their functions to serve the body as a whole. This reminder will serve church staff members well. The fruitfulness of their ministry and the ministry of the church as a whole depend on it.

One of the greatest tools for clarity with the church staff is a weekly meeting structured by a deliberate agenda. Staff meetings do not have to be long to be effective. They do have to be well prepared and agenda driven so that they do not waste valuable time by many, especially part-time employees. If a pastor ever needs an incentive to make time to prepare the agenda or do the prework that leads to a fruitful meeting, one might calculate the hourly cost to the church of gathering staff members together. No matter what size staff the church employs, it costs money in time dedicated to the meeting for them to assemble. With good preparations, these meetings are measured in minutes. When the time is unplanned and uncoordinated, they are measured in hours. The balance is to meet long enough to inform, plan, encourage, and motivate one another and to meet in a short enough timeframe to honor the value of everyone's time.

The agenda may include the following:

- Devotional sharing and prayer time for the staff members and church
- Celebration of the ways that God is working in the congregation
- Announcements or a brief listing of upcoming events and the schedule of the week
- Agenda items including the ministry initiatives discussed by the governing board that will guide the work of the staff as they live out the vision in a variety of areas. Agenda items should be determined before the meeting so that all parties are prepared. New items that arise go on a future agenda.

The weekly staff meeting is the forum in which the pastor is able to connect staff members who do not attend the meetings of the governing board to the plans on which the board acts throughout the year. The staff meeting is also a place for discerning the work of the Holy Spirit in relation to the true benefits and costs of ministry initiatives. The staff can then ask whether the goals shared with the governing board need expansion or adjustment so that they can be both faithful and fruitful.

The pastor needs to hear the insights and expertise of staff members and share information with them in an organized fashion so that staff will be key allies in their common work. Paul's metaphor of the human body remains so relevant for the church today because anyone in leadership can see the interconnections of all ministry areas with one another. Fruitfulness of the various parts contributes to fruitfulness of the whole.

Consider the benefits that clarity will bring to a church staff:

- Mutuality: When staff members understand the rationale for allocating scarce resources in certain ways, they are better able to celebrate the use of the funds instead of competing for them.
- Influence: People often ask church staff about ministry areas that have nothing to do with their staff work on the assumption that staff know all things. The more informed they are, the better they are able to field questions and point to the right sources of information for more details. An informed staff communicates to the laity that everything happens aboveboard. The smaller the staff, the more

important this becomes. It is also true for every staff position. A church secretary who understands the mission and vision of the church has the ability to build a positive rationale for the work of the church in the numerous conversations in a given week.

- Justice: Church staff members typically work for low salaries and often give extra hours to their ministry. It is good and right to let them know what is going on and why.

The Congregation

The final and most essential group that must experience clarity around the church's vision and key initiatives is the congregation. This is the most important group to address and the most difficult to keep adequately informed. No matter what the church size, success in effective communication with the congregation will seem elusive. Several available options assist leaders in this task. Leaders should employ multiple ways to communicate with and seek input from members of the congregation.

Organizing focus groups whenever the church governing board is working on long-range planning or other major decisions is one method. These groups are limited to twenty to twenty-five persons per group. Multiple groups are offered and meet at different times, including morning, afternoon, and evening so that as many members as possible can attend, given their personal schedules and preferences. The focus group leader offers a clearly stated concept that the group can discuss. It is a time for considering, questioning, and improving concepts. Focus groups occur before making decisions so that leaders can understand what concerns the idea may raise or what enthusiasm it may engender from church members. These groups are often held prior to key votes that would lead to financial commitments or changes to the priorities of the church's ministry. The feedback they provide often perfects the plans brought back to the governing board or congregation for a vote.

It is important that observers not closely connected to the topic under discussion record good notes from the focus groups. Some use two reporters for each gathering. The comments and observations collected from all the groups provide a valuable resource for pastor, staff, and governing board. It is amazing how patterns emerge in such focus groups and clues emerge from the congregation.

It is true that much work goes into such meetings, so it is wise to reserve this strategy for major initiatives that affect the entire congregation. Otherwise, the process will lose interest and participation. The value of these groups is that they give members of the church knowledge of plans, a forum to ask questions, and the ability to share their perspectives. If the topic under consideration requires significant financial resources, these people ultimately will be asked to supply the money. Encouraging their participation from the beginning, before deciding anything, provides the opportunity for the congregation to get excited about great ideas and to express their concern about ideas that need more thought.

The Pastor's E-mail or *E-note* is a means of providing the church with information in a bite-sized form on a weekly basis. Written in the pastor's voice, this e-mail should feel more like a personal communication from the pastor than a list of announcements from the church. If the church uses e-mail for the weekly activities, that notice can go to the congregation at another time during the week.

The goal of the pastor's e-mail is to give people a behind-the-scenes look at the church and its ministry. The reason people read this e-mail so regularly is that it gives a sense of relationship between them and their pastor. The personality of the pastor must come through in the style and voice of this communication. This communication will take time to craft each week, but it is a chance for the pastor to share insights regarding the life of the church and the impact of its ministry that will motivate and encourage its members. It allows the pastor to set the tone of the church's narrative and to give good information. It can be used to encourage people to sign up for events or volunteer for upcoming ministries. But it must never simply become a list of announcements. A line or two from the pastor that explains why he or she finds these to be important to growth in discipleship or beneficial to the community should accompany the events that the communication promotes. It is an opportunity to connect every activity to the congregation's vision.[1]

Vision Sunday is an annual event when the pastor speaks to the congregation about the key initiatives that the governing board has adopted. The Vision Sunday sermon should be primarily motivational and secondarily informational. Biblically grounded, it helps the congregation clearly understand what fruit the church hopes to harvest in the coming year. The rest of the worship service needs to include inspirational music and broad participation by a variety of age groups. Design the service in such a way that people leave the sanctuary surprised by the joy and inspiration they experience when they think of the future of their church.

Annual Report Dinner(s) are beneficial in the fall when church activity is picking up after the summer months. During these dinners, share an annual report of the accomplishments of the church over the past year and invite discussion. This is primarily a time of appreciation and motivation. The pastor can give thanks to God and to the church members who gave time and money generously. Michael Slaughter provides a wonderful guide to these meetings along with planning timelines and suggestions for content.[2] The key to these meetings is to treat attendees as honored guests who have enabled the fruitfulness of the church's ministry over the past year. The church, unlike almost every other non-profit organization, is often guilty of underappreciating key leaders, volunteers, and donors. The Annual Dinner should offer very simple fare for the meal. It should be generous in its appreciation of everyone who attends. This event highlights not the talents and gifts of the few but the contributions of the many that make the church fruitful each week.

This is another relationship-building opportunity for the pastor, who should also talk about the vision, the year ahead, and the fruit the church hopes to yield. A time of questions and answers can follow the pastor's remarks. If the hope of Vision Sunday is to have a high "wow factor" that may include great visuals and stirring music, the goal of the Annual Dinner is to express appreciation for members of the congregation and inspire them with the picture of what lies ahead in the coming year. The pastor should consider how these purposes will affect his or her approach when talking at the dinner and the planning for the event in general. A printed annual report summarizing the accomplishments of the church over the past year as well as plans for the year ahead enables people to recall the celebration and share information with those who could not attend. It also provides members of your congregation with information to share with friends or neighbors whom they want to invite to the church.

There are many options for bringing clarity about the vision to the congregation. All work to the same benefits:

- Transparency: Good information takes power away from people pursuing personal agendas. Good communication is like a fan that clears the air of the haze of rumor that often accumulates in church parking lots.

- Celebration: So often pastors and congregations spend time solving problems rather than celebrating the fruits of ministry that please the heart of God. It is a source of encouragement to everyone when the church can share joy about what the Spirit of God is doing in our midst and how God is using our church to bless the community.
- Stewardship: These people make the vision possible through their giving. They need to know the vision of the congregation and how it is being lived. Then they will be encouraged to give generously. This happens only when they trust that the church is a good steward of their gifts.
- Conflict resolution: Leaders regularly resolve misunderstandings and differences that arise in the normal flow of congregational life. Communicating appropriately with the congregation about such matters through a variety of means acknowledges the inevitable conflicts that arise in the church as important and in need of attention. Reassuring others that such problems are being addressed enables everyone to keep moving toward other initiatives.

The types of structures and processes here are especially important in a church experiencing growth in fruitful ministry. In the winter of 2010, the Washington, D.C., area was hit by a record snowstorm. More than thirty inches of snow fell in a two-day period. Children and adults were excited by the snow. News of the weather was all the television carried for two straight days. The snowstorm was an adventure. It also brought property damage and power outages. Healthy trees toppled. Branches broke and fell over power lines. Roofs in good condition began to sag and even collapse. Gutters were clogged so that homes experienced water damage from ice that crept inside and then thawed. The problem was not that homes were poorly built or trees were sick. They had survived many snowstorms in the past. The reason so much damage occurred was that this snowstorm left more than two and one-half feet of snow at one time. The structures simply were not built for the load they now carried.

If your church experiences a fruitful ministry, it will be exciting. It will also create a new burden of opportunity that you must deal with organizationally. If you design processes and structures that will carry the load that fruitfulness will generate, you will be able to enjoy the excitement of what is happening in your church without the fear of impending collapse.

CONCLUSION

Often church vision casting and goal setting are nothing more than a fireworks show. After the light dissipates and the smoke clears, little remains but the memory of a great meeting or retreat. It is always easier to dream of what might be than to work month after month to bring God's dream for the church into a new reality. If vision discernment and goal setting are to bear fruit that benefits the church and the community, the ongoing conversation about key initiatives is essential. Well-planned structures and processes are crucial.

Each church will develop its own processes that are sensitive to the particular culture of the congregation and the community. But the culture must carry the vision if it is to bear fruit. Finally, the image of fruitfulness applies to the systems used by the church as well. Today's well-planned structures and processes will need to be periodically reviewed to ensure they continue to achieve their purpose. These processes will need to be tended, pruned, and grown if they are to remain healthy for the church over time.

CHAPTER EIGHT

SUSTAINING FRUITFUL LEADERSHIP: LEARNING TO LEAD YOURSELF

A ll that we have learned about fruitfulness is unlikely to become real in a congregation unless a pastoral leader discovers what it means to lead yourself.

A few years ago, Tom's wife, Karen, woke up with a desire to run a marathon.

> I don't really understand why anyone wants to run a marathon. If you ever think you want to run one, I would suggest that you go to a marathon and see the finish line. It isn't pretty. At the Marine Corps Marathon in Washington, D.C., they have a whole tent at the finish line for the wounded. Marines carry downed runners into the first aid tent on stretchers to give them liquids or rub the cramps out of their legs. I was both proud and relieved to see my wife run toward the finish line of this 26.2-mile race.

Fruitful leadership can be seen as a "change marathon." This type of ministry is a distance event. You cannot sprint and successfully reach the finish line. The distance between where a church begins the race and the fruitful ministry it hopes to achieve can be a long journey. The cumulative impact of the steps necessary to traverse the distance will affect the leader over time. The leader must consider how to run the race so that he or she can cross the finish line without the assistance of a stretcher.

Marathon runners are familiar with the phrase "hitting the wall." This period of fatigue and energy loss happens after the body depletes its first round of energy and then taps into the glycogen that is stored in the liver and muscles. Glycogen is the secondary store of energy used by the body when it is under unusual exertion or stress. The exertion of endurance athletes requires the extra energy that glycogen provides. As the marathon continues, glycogen stores in the liver and muscles are depleted, and performance drops. The runner has hit the wall.

The critical issue for marathon runners is to deal with the problem of energy depletion by finding ways to restore themselves even as the race continues. Runners may choose from a host of products that they often carry in bottles attached to their belts. During the race, they are very attentive to how much water they carry with them and where water will be offered along the course. They understand that if they do not rejuvenate their bodies in such ways, they cannot successfully complete the marathon.

Similarly, the exertion required to move a church into fruitful ministry will claim the energy of the leader. Moving a church toward a culture of high commitment and vitality will take its toll. Managing change can be exhilarating, but it is always taxing. The toll it takes on the leader can lead to spiritual, emotional, and physical exhaustion. Spiritual leaders, like endurance athletes, know what it means to hit the wall and feel that they simply cannot go any farther on the journey. Unlike the exhaustion felt by endurance athletes, the exhaustion of spiritual leadership is much more difficult to discern.

One of the best examples of the exhaustion that ministry can bring is found in the record of the prophet Elijah's life in 1 Kings. Elijah was trying to turn Israel to the Lord during the reign of King Ahab, a man who was deeply influenced by his wife, Jezebel. Under her leadership, Ahab had encouraged Israel to turn to the worship of Baal and Asherah. He had allowed Jezebel to kill the Lord's prophets. Elijah confronts the king and asks him to bring the prophets of Baal and Asherah to Mount Carmel along with the people of Israel. The prophets of Baal are not able to summon their god to produce fire for a sacrifice, but the Lord provides so much fire from heaven that it consumes an altar flooded with water. The people show their loyalty to the Lord by putting the prophets of Baal to death.

One would think that Elijah would be so convinced of God's power and would be so hopeful that the people would show their loyalty to God that he would be ready to rise to the next challenge. Instead, Elijah hits the wall.

When a messenger tells him that Jezebel wants him dead, the scripture tells us, "Elijah was afraid and ran for his life" (1 Kings 19:3 NIV). Rather than confront an idolatrous queen of Israel in the strength of the Lord, Elijah runs into the wilderness and hides. There he sits under a broom tree and prays that he might die. He articulates a thought that has entered the minds of many fruitful leaders: "I have had enough, LORD" (1 Kings 19:4 NIV).

Pastors and other leaders of fruitful congregations will recognize a pattern to the leadership cycle.

First one hears the clarity of calling and vision from the Lord and recognizes the resources provided by the Holy Spirit. This is followed by a time of ministry when plans are executed, problems are solved, and other problems are faced. Often this is the period of the greatest accomplishments in ministry. It is a time when excitement in the church is palpable and people find great vitality to their faith. One would think that this would lead to an extended period of fruitfulness and growth in which the leader would flourish in the face of the problems that are inevitable in the life of the church.

Unfortunately, there is a wall that many leaders hit, and they begin to feel weary. "I have had enough, Lord," is not just a quotation in the Bible. Many have uttered that during what appeared to be their finest hours in ministry. Fruitful leaders must recognize that they have to attend to the replenishment of their physical, emotional, and spiritual health. If they do so, they will experience an upward spiral to deeper reliance upon the Lord, growth in problem-solving skills, and the reassurance of faith in a powerful God. This path leads to a renewed clarity of calling and vision that will bring the next level of provision and competency for future leadership.

Likewise, if leaders do not attend to the replenishment of energy, they will experience a downward spiral in ways that can be tragic. Leaders who were once passionate become comfortable with the status quo. Leaders who were once hopeful about the future become cynical about the work of the church and its people. Those who once enjoyed riding the flow of God's power find themselves stuck on the dry banks of self-reliance. The godly pursue pleasures of the flesh. The vines of fruitful ministry begin to produce only sour grapes.

Staying Connected to the Vine

> We remain connected to the vine because that is the way we bear fruit. And here the inward spiritual grace becomes an outward and visible sign. The natural consequence of a healthy root taking in nutrients is that it produces something wonderful. It bears fruit.[1]
> Kenneth H. Carter Jr.

Most spiritual leaders can describe periods when they hit the wall in ministry, even when everything looked fine to outsiders. Not long ago the church Tom serves finished a seven-year building and relocation process necessitated by the growth of the congregation. On Sunday mornings, three different buildings were used for Sunday school. Often there was only standing room during Sunday worship. The staff had grown, and everyone was looking forward to moving to the new facility. Local outreach had expanded to new heights, and a new Spanish language service was planned.

At the height of all these blessings the church endured the tragic deaths of four members in quick succession. Tom had been involved with most of these families in a variety of circumstances and knew some of them as friends.

During that three-month period, between the grief I felt as I ministered to those families and the leadership challenges of our growing congregation, I knew that something was happening to me internally. It was sometime later that I was surprised to realize that I had hit the wall that marathon runners anticipate.

The symptoms were not hard to see in retrospect. Ministry became automated. I could hear people's concerns, but I was not as compassionate as I had been in the past. I was internally short-tempered with our leaders and my staff colleagues. I was frustrated everywhere I went: at the office, at home, in traffic, and in the community. I was often sullen in the evenings. Two things caught my attention. My wife told me that one of my best traits was joy, and it had been a long time since she had seen it: "Has it occurred to you that you are depressed?" The other was the day my daughter saw me react to a fellow driver with frustration. She looked at me and said with great concern, "Dad, the thing I am wondering is why you are always so angry lately."

To an outsider, things could not have seemed better. The church relocation was complete. Our congregation was vital and enthusiastic. God had clearly blessed our ministry. The congregation consistently surrounded the bereaved families in love. Inside my mind, however, I was praying Elijah's prayer: *Lord, I have had enough.*

In their book *Pain: The Gift Nobody Wants*, Philip Yancey and Paul Brand make a convincing argument that the ability to experience pain is a gift that God gives us to keep us from deeper harm.[2] Dr. Brand worked for many years with people in India afflicted with leprosy. His observations about those living with the disease helped the medical community understand that leprosy destroys the nerves that enable humans to experience pain. When the disease progressed to the point that patients no longer felt pain when they burned or cut themselves, they began to experience multiple wounds that could lead to the loss of limbs or life-threatening infections. Pain, which most people consider a burden to avoid, is actually the gift that enables us to understand the boundaries of healthy living.

Spiritual leaders must pay attention to the painful parts of the leadership cycle if they are to run the race with perseverance and see the fulfillment of their calling. But we can learn from marathon training. Some of the principles followed by endurance athletes are easily transferred into the marathon journey of fruitful leadership. Here are some disciplines that would be a blessing if they were built into the lives of fruitful leaders:

1. Take Time to Stretch

Runners stretch before and after they run so that their muscles can be prepared and then recover from use. Serious runners understand that this habit is nonnegotiable if they are to successfully train without injury. Without proper stretching, muscles will not function well over any distance.

Spiritual leaders must consider what habits are basic to their physical, emotional, and spiritual health. While this may seem obvious, multiple studies show that clergy struggle more than other professional groups with such self-care issues. Commitment to calling and stress of ministry often lead pastors to neglect habits that are basic to the health of the Christian life. Time is not allocated to exercise. Sleep is minimal. Scripture is read for sermon preparation but not for personal edification. Work hours increase while time with family diminishes. Attention to healthy eating habits is lost to fast food to fuel a hectic schedule.

Notice what God did for Elijah during his period in the desert. The first command of God's angel does not sound particularly spiritual:

"Get up and eat." He looked around, and there by his head was a cake of bread baked over hot coals, and a jar of water. He ate and drank and then lay down again.

The angel of the LORD came back a second time and touched him and said, "Get up and eat, for the journey is too much for you." So he got up and ate and drank. Strengthened by that food, he traveled forty days and forty nights until he reached Horeb, the mountain of God. There he went into a cave and spent the night. (1 Kings 19:5-9 NIV)

God's first order of business for the depleted prophet was to restore basic habits of health. I am always surprised when I read those words. God does not tell Elijah to go back to the scrolls of the Law or deepen his prayer life. Our Creator knows that we have to start with the basics. "Get up. Eat. Drink. Sleep." Attention to physical health is integral to the recovery of emotional and spiritual health.

Volumes stress the importance of church leaders maintaining their spiritual lives. The foundations of the spiritual disciplines are essential for those who would attempt to pursue God's vision in their church and world. But attention to spiritual disciplines alone is unlikely to sustain the well-being and fruitfulness of church leaders. Health data related to clergy illustrate there is now a crisis of our physical and emotional life that requires attention if the church is to live faithfully and fruitfully over time.

Rather than provide a powerful alternative lifestyle that can be clearly seen by those who do not know Christ, the physical health of many church leaders is a reflection of the culture in which they reside as it relates to weight, diet, and the necessity for multiple medications to attend to health issues that are a result of stress and poor health habits. The disciplines related to the care of one's body such as food, rest, exercise, and renewal are as spiritual and as necessary as the care of one's soul.

Clearly, God desires us to have health in all areas of life, from the renewing of the mind, attention to matters of the heart, and the care of the body as a temple of the Holy Spirit. Often these matters are discussed under the umbrella of *self-care*. This term might be counterproductive for church leaders, who often consider *self-anything* as selfish. Church leaders should understand that attention to physical and emotional well-being is a matter of stewardship of the greatest resources that God has given us: the body and the mind. It is the will of God that we experience the health, vitality, and joy that come when we care for the human body that God took time to craft and provide with unique gifts for helping to bring in God's reign.

2. Move at the Pace of Your Success

When you train for a marathon, you don't start by thinking about twenty-six miles, especially if you have not run that far before. First you learn to run two to three miles. Then you get to the point that two to three miles are not a problem, and you think about four to six miles. And four to six miles become seven to eight miles, which lead to nine to ten miles, and soon we are talking about some serious distance.

Anxiety about a fulfilled vision for ministry can wear out a good leader. When the church begins to feel vital and commitment is on the rise, it can become addictive. As objectives and goals are accomplished, leaders naturally begin to think about the next big thing. What would we look like in ten more years? How much more building do we need to do? How many more staff do we need to hire? Could we handle the ministry load of the additional people projected to arrive with the opening of the new facility? It does not take long to realize that the journey that brought the leader to this point of vitality has been taxing. Thinking of the steps necessary to move to the final summit can feel crushing. This is why the leader must focus on the steps necessary to move to the next summit.

Another bit of related advice that new marathon runners receive is to be sure to consider the whole course. The course is not the same everywhere. The Boston Marathon has Heartbreak Hill, where many runners hit their wall. You have to manage your energy and not run full throttle as though every stage of the marathon required the same amount of energy.

Wise leaders know the difference between the hills and the flat areas in ministry. These cannot be run with the same intensity. One requires effort while the other offers the opportunity for recovery. The leader who never slows down through the ups and downs of the ministry season will be ill prepared for the most challenging parts of the course.

Tom learned the importance of this lesson through experience.

The summer after I hit the ministry wall, our church was supposed to begin construction of our new sanctuary. Prior to the completion of phase one, our church had placed phase two on a timeline that required us to begin work as soon as we moved. As we interviewed stewardship consultants for this effort, I heard all that would be expected of the senior pastor. I knew that I had just come off one long and tall hill and did not have the energy to tackle another. Initially, I felt embarrassed to tell the church council that I didn't have the energy to pull it off. My desire was to use the summer to recuperate from the last two years. I said that I wanted to go on a mission trip, take two weeks of vacation, and then take a few days to get my daughter settled in college. I wanted to be goal-less for a season. I asked if we could defer phase two for a year. I was shocked when other leaders on our church council expressed their gratitude for my honesty. They, too, were tired from the work of the last two years. They also wanted a break but felt guilty expressing this need. One man later told me that he had planned to resign from leadership but, after hearing that we were going to delay this next big effort, was willing to continue in service.

Knowing when to exert extra energy and when to slow down is a key skill in completing the race.

3. Be Discerning about Pain

Runners know that pain goes with the territory. The question they learn to ask about pain is whether it is normal pain that they need to push through or whether the body is telling them to pull over and attend to something deeper.

Aren't you still surprised when ministry is difficult? When people complain or say untrue things about you or the church? Caught off guard when key leaders don't get along? Dumbfounded when problems don't resolve quickly and easily? Warning: if you are going to try and move the established church to fruitfulness and to vitality and commitment, you will endure pain in the process.

Because pain is normal to fruitful ministry, it is essential that we do not create unnecessary pain. One pastor hit the wall one day and got out of ministry. He regularly created his own pain. Once he was serving a small country church and wanted the congregation to celebrate Communion by intinction. He felt strongly about the symbolism involved in sharing a common loaf and a common cup. They said they were not interested. They loved their old Communion service with its individual cups. He did it anyway. Many refused to take Communion. He tried to inspire them by giving the church a beautiful plate and goblet. The trustees refused his gift.

As the pastor, he had authority to make this change. Any professor of worship would agree that the symbolism he wanted them to experience properly conveyed the meaning of Holy Communion. But the question he should have asked was: "Is it worth the pain?" Make sure the possible fruitfulness is worth the pain. Fruitful leaders understand where pain is worth it and where it is not.

If you discern that possible fruitfulness is worth the pain, prepare yourself to cope with the pain without breaking. Marathon runners develop a skill that would benefit church leaders. They learn to discern normal pain that they can run through from injury pain that requires special attention and care. There are times to pull over and attend to pain that feels like it may signal a problem that will have long-term consequences. This may include engaging the services of a competent pastoral counselor. There are seasons in life when we can be blessed by a new spiritual discipline. For some this can come through sessions with a counselor, spiritual director, or coach. Having someone listen to you without interruptions and with complete confidentiality can be a blessing. Like a physical therapist dealing with an injury, the right professional counselor can help you find ways to pursue spiritual health.

It is important for church leaders, and pastors in particular, to remember that engaging a counselor or coach is something that healthy people do. Unhealthy people go the course alone, rely on their own instincts when they are feeling pain, and do not seek the counsel of others. The Bible speaks often of the importance of seeking wisdom from others. Pastors may find this difficult since they see themselves as those to whom others come for guidance. Pastors often refer others to a counselor but may secretly feel a sense of failure when they seek such assistance for themselves. Time with a counselor, spiritual director, or coach may often be the means of grace that God desires for faithful servants who have listened to so many but rarely had the opportunity to share their concerns and aspirations for ministry and life.

Runners learn that a certain amount of pain accompanies the sport. But other kinds of pain, if left unattended, will bring injury that can end races and careers altogether.

4. Make Time for Recovery

Runners build recovery into their workout routines. Jim Loehr and Tony Schwartz in *The Power of Full Engagement*[3] discuss their studies of top athletes to understand why some people are peak performers and others are not. The difference in the top professional tennis players, they found, was not in preparation or tactics on the court. The most significant difference between the top athletes and the lower-performing ones had to do with what they did with the seconds between points. Top athletes have disciplined habits of recovery. They have rituals of resting between points, games, and matches that allow their minds and bodies to maximize rest and refuel.

When a pastor reports not having taken a vacation in years, it is likely that pastor is not healthy. Chances are, little joy of the Lord will be found in this pastor's experience. If a spiritual leader is not careful, periods of great fruitfulness in ministry can lead to the mind-set of indispensability and the lack of joy that accompanies it. Soon you are not having fun, and you are not fun to be around. You become a joy vacuum, sucking happiness and joy out of every room you enter. Life has become serious business with no respite.

Recovery is essential to spiritual leaders because they often work long hours with emotionally toxic materials. Then they move to engage challenges, and consensus must be built with a variety of individuals and teams. No hazardous materials team would be allowed to work such long shifts without stopping for a time of replenishment.

The key is to plan and schedule recovery time and consider it the spiritual discipline of sabbath. Church leaders who are on a mission from God tend to violate the sabbath more than any other part of their interior life. There are many ways to find replenishment. Some take minutes while others take days. Which of the following help you feel renewed?

1. Vacation
2. Time with family
3. Time with renewing friends
4. Continuing education that is enjoyable in content and location
5. Mission trips that include adventures and people you enjoy
6. Special projects that sound interesting
7. A study week to read or plan sermons
8. Phone calls to friends
9. Other?

Take some time to consider what best renews your body and spirit. Then put such things on your calendar. It is essential to remember that you are as important in God's eyes as the people to whom you minister.

5. Find a Cheering Section

When Tom's wife, Karen, was running the Marine Corps Marathon, her family moved around the course to cheer her on at three separate locations. She said the most difficult part of the race was the Fourteenth Street Bridge. It was around mile eighteen. She told Tom later, "I was getting tired. It looked twelve miles long."

People around her were beginning to drop out. One man was cursing the marathon, cursing his training, cursing his body, cursing his intellect. He was in bad shape. He was dropping out. Karen said she suddenly felt tempted to drop out as well.

Tom asked her why that leg of the race was so hard. She said, "They don't allow the crowd on the bridge. You lose your cheering section."

Long before Elijah confronted the prophets of Baal, he was struggling with King Ahab and Queen Jezebel. That conflict was made all the more difficult by Elijah's assumption that he was alone. He believed himself to be one of the last prophets of the Lord. One day the Spirit led him to another faithful prophet, Obadiah, who gave him good news:

> I your servant have worshiped the LORD since my youth. Haven't you heard, my lord, what I did while Jezebel was killing the prophets of the LORD? I hid a hundred of the LORD's prophets in two caves, fifty in each, and supplied them with food and water. (1 Kings 18:12b-13 NIV)

Think of how different Elijah's outlook would have been had he been able to interact with just a few of the Lord's prophets who were hidden in those caves. Few things are more discouraging than the feeling of isolation that comes when you find yourself alone.

Whom have you enlisted to be in your cheering section?

These people have to include more than your family. As important as they are, they can't cover enough of the course.

Three groups can prove indispensable when things get difficult:

1. Friends who are spiritual leaders
2. Friends who value you as a person rather than as a pastor
3. Staff members and leaders in your church who share your calling and care about your journey

The encouragement they bring can make all the difference in finishing the race well. This cheering section provides support in three primary ways:

1. Encouragement: These people pray for you and are generous with conversation that reminds you of your unique talents and giftedness.

2. Accountability: Empower them to ask you hard questions about your personal habits, spiritual life, and vocational pursuits. They must be able to ask the question behind the question. They must ask not only, "What is your main vocational goal?" but also, "Is this to serve God or your own pursuits?"

3. Insight: These people know you and understand the Christian life. Talking with them enables you to understand your situation better, whether it is a leadership issue at your church or a sin that is drawing you away from the way of Christ.

The cheering section is the place you go when you are tempted to give up the race. We have grown accustomed, especially in the West, to believe that attention to our life in Christ is typically a solitary pursuit of prayer, Scripture study, and other disciplines such as fasting and meditation that are often personal in nature. There is another truth that must be heard. If we are to pursue a vital ministry, we must enjoy regular experiences of community that renew us. Here is a principle for spiritual leaders that is often neglected: we need cave time. This is not time for an individual leader to go into a cave for personal reflection or emotional isolation. It is time in the cave with those who share their passion and aspirations for the church. If Elijah could have enjoyed some cave time with the prophets gathered there, he would have found his burdens lifted and his soul encouraged.

6. Remember the Dream

Karen has three goals for her marathon: finish, finish by old time, or finish by an improved time. She is truly happy meeting any of these goals. One thing that she likes about running is that it is not about anybody else's time. She doesn't concern herself if others pass her, and she does not feel better if she passes others. She is able to celebrate the accomplishments of those who finish before her and encourage the hard work of those who come in after her. A new personal record would be nice, but she always remembers that when she started, she just wanted to finish well.

There is a lesson here. Fruitfulness in the church is not strengthened through a sense of competition with other pastors or churches. There is, rather, a flow of vitality from God's Spirit when we are able to celebrate all that God is doing with our lives while we also celebrate what God is doing in the lives of others. Runners at a marathon do not compete with one another as much as they propel one another along the course. While a few runners are hoping to win or place in the top ten of the marathon, most people simply want to finish or beat their personal best time. Because everyone recognizes what an accomplishment it is simply to finish the race, marathon runners typically train together, share insights, and celebrate one another's accomplishments. During the race, every person's desire to finish creates a momentum and flow that bless all the runners in the marathon. In this way the runners are both striving for their best time and desiring the best for one another. The reign of God would be well served if pastors and churches could embrace these values of the marathon runner.

When we start in ministry, we usually do not have grand goals for recognition or achievement. We want to be a good pastor. We want to be used by God. More than ever, we want to finish well. We want to finish with a heart of greater love. We want to have a joyful countenance. We want to be persons who easily extend grace and forgiveness. We want to do the things that God is blessing and be guided by the Spirit of the living God. We want to fight the good fight, finish the race, and keep the faith. We have come to realize that if we are going to help the church move through fruitful change into God's future, the most important people we will have to lead are ourselves.

CHAPTER NINE

PLANTING, WATERING, AND PRAYING FOR GROWTH

I planted the seed, Apollos watered it, but God made it grow.
(1 Corinthians 3:6 NIV)

Throughout our Scriptures, the people of God are called to be fruit-ful. We have mined some of the rich images from Genesis through Revelation, and we have discovered many tools and skills that will help us become fruitful leaders. It is tempting to believe that if we do all these good things, a rich harvest is guaranteed. But those who tend the apple orchards know otherwise. As the apostle Paul reminded the Corinthians, fruitfulness finally is in God's hands.

Conversely, while Paul knew well that God gives the growth, he cul-tivated in himself and others the skills of planting and watering. Paul may have been the most fruitful leader in the history of Christian disci-ple making. Clergy and lay leaders are stewards of the garden, and we are accountable for doing our work both faithfully and fruitfully.

Throughout the history of our church, some have forgotten one part or the other of Paul's truth and have stumbled into what the church has called heresy. To hold these two parts together will always be our diffi-cult but necessary challenge.

FAITHFUL AND FRUITFUL

> Occasionally someone argues, "God desires faithfulness, not fruitfulness." Whoever suggests this might benefit from an evening of study with a Bible and a concordance, looking up references to fruit, harvest, sowing, vines, and seeds. Fruitfulness is clearly expected of Christian disciples. Jesus' teachings consistently present the expectation that his followers are stewards and that when God has entrusted them with something, God expects them to return what has been entrusted and more. . . .
>
> Fruitfulness and faithfulness are not mutually exclusive. If the only way to remain faithful is to devalue fruitfulness, or worse, if fruitfulness indicates lack of faithfulness, then where does this take us in our thinking? Then the crowds who gathered to hear the Sermon on the Mount and the five thousand who waited all day for Jesus to break bread would prove Jesus' unfaithfulness, providing evidence that he was pandering, compromising, and watering down the gospel.[1]
>
> Robert Schnase

TENDING THE ORCHARD: PLANTING AND WATERING

Those who tend the apple orchard know there will always be factors that are out of their control. Still they use every skill they have learned to work toward a rich harvest. Their livelihood depends upon it. Workers in God's vineyard still have much to learn from them.

KEEPERS OF THE VISION

The tender of an orchard needs a vision of what a healthy tree and a healthy orchard look like. A casual observer might see a new seedling; the orchard worker can see a full-grown, vibrant apple tree laden with fruit. That vision guides all the care and attention of those trees through their life span. Like faithful orchard workers, fruitful church leaders must be the primary keepers of the vision. We must be able to see what others in the body of Christ do not see, hope what they cannot yet hope, and long for what they do not know can exist. Fruitful church leaders must be so connected to God that all efforts are directed toward the fruition of God's vision, never forgetting Jesus' warning that "apart from me you can do nothing" (John 15:5).

GIVING ATTENTION TO THE HARVEST

The tender of the apple orchard gives attention to the harvest. Have we done our tending this year in a way that has led to a plentiful harvest? The owner of the orchard will ask for an accounting. How many bushels? Is the fruit healthy? The owner will find it peculiar if the steward of the orchard has not paid attention to the quantity and quality of the harvest.

How much more accountable for the harvest are we as fruitful leaders in the church. It is not apples for which we are responsible but beloved children of God. Is it not peculiar when some do not find it important to pay attention to the richness of *this* harvest?

Fruitful church leaders know one manifestation of the Holy Spirit in the early church was numerical growth, and they look at the growth of worship attendance and membership. They also know that numerical growth must always be coupled with the health of Christian discipleship that includes a deeper experience of loving community and a deeper pursuit of holiness. They pay attention to how many adults are in small groups and participate in Christian outreach. They view the stewardship of the church as a function of its discipleship rather than wealth. They also have a feel for the spiritual climate of the church. Fruitful leaders long for the transformation of the church in those areas that evidence Christian discipleship.

Bishop Hope Morgan Ward in a communication to church leaders reports the number of members in churches where she serves and then asks, "But, who's counting?" She answers, "God is counting, that's who. The Bible tells us so." In the first chapter of Acts, for example, Peter stands up among the believers, a group numbering about 120 (1:15). In the next chapter, after Peter's sermon at Pentecost, "about three thousand persons were added" (2:41). Day by day the Lord "added to their number those who were being saved" (2:47). By chapter 4, the believers "numbered about five thousand" (4:4). And after

Saul's conversion in chapter 9, the author describes a spiritually vital church that "increased in numbers" (9:31). Numbers *are* significant in Acts—for they were the numbers of those hearing the good news for the first time.

A pastor's tongue-in-cheek parody captured the question of numbers in a stark way.[2] Pastor Tim Stevens tells about going on vacation when his three children were quite young. The entire family was standing in a crowded hotel lobby in a big city when, to his surprise, he saw one of their children, a three-year-old, in an elevator going skyward, her nose pressed to the glass with fright on her face. *What am I to do?* the pastor thought. *Nothing,* was his reply. After all, two out of the three children were still there. And after all, there were many things he and his wife had not yet done with the remaining two children. Maybe they should focus more on having a deeper relationship with the two remaining children. In fact, this pastor had never really been a numbers person. He was not the kind of pastor who, if he came to the end of a vacation with fewer children than at the beginning of the vacation, would feel guilty about the negative numbers. "I'm just not into the numbers game," the pastor insisted.

This story should remind us that when we end a year with two children fewer on our Sunday school rolls, they are someone's children. Or when a campus ministry adds numbers to its participants, each of those students is someone's child. The world is full of children alone on elevators, and each is a child for whom Christ died. They are the numbers a fruitful leader seeks.

One need not claim that the number of persons coming to church is everything (a position that virtually no one defends) to recognize that many churches demonstrate little sense of responsibility for the number of lives left untouched by God's love in their communities. Both qualitative and quantitative measures of church vitality have their place in any useful ministry audit. Leadership that does not insist on careful monitoring of such measures is unlikely to be fruitful.

Conventional wisdom in the last generation resisted numerical goals and said leaders should concentrate instead on improving the internal life of the church. However, it may be that we will not make the right internal changes needed to reach new people until we first *commit* to reaching new people. When we commit ourselves, for example, to reaching younger people and more diverse people, our willingness to be accountable for such outcomes will lead us to discover what we need to do to accomplish them. We will be led to engage the people we seek to reach to learn of their needs and to understand the nature of their quest for God. We can then shape worship and ministries in ways that will speak to those we are committed to reaching for Christ. Our congregational life will be shaped by the mission to which we are committed.

WHY COUNT?

British sociologist and ethicist Robin Gill tells about his experience on the speaking circuit in England lecturing about the importance of numbers:

Whenever I go to conferences to talk about strategies for church growth, there are always two people in the audience. I am almost convinced that they are the same two people who follow me around the country.

I always make a point of starting with God. My understanding of church growth starts from worship; it is theologically based. Yet, when I have finished speaking after the usual 55 minutes, a rather aggressive hand always goes up. And exactly the same question follows each time: "When are you going to bring God into all of this?"

A mixture of points follows this rhetorical question. Some of them go straight to the Holy Ghost—less often to the Holy Spirit. If I truly believed in the Holy Ghost, I would not worry about strategies for church growth, or, indeed, about strategies for anything very much.

The other person to object is much more languorous. Typically, one ankle is placed on the other thigh, hands are interlocked behind the neck, and the ubiquitous plastic chair is at a 45-degree angle. So far, this person has never tipped over, but he does always go straight for the anatomy: "Why do you keep going on about bums on seats?"

Frankly, I never mention xxxx on seats except, of course, in reported speech. I was much too well brought up for that. Yet, this chap—it is always a chap—keeps bringing them up, whenever I speak.

So, why am I so obsessed? Why am I so obsessed that, when I speak for those 55 minutes, this man in the audience gets so annoyed with my findings that he forgets that I started with God? My obsessions get such predictable reactions that you would think that I might learn one day. Learn simply to forget about all this church growth stuff. Learn to accept decline like everyone else.[3]

AND GOD MADE IT GROW

Fruitful leaders are attentive to the harvest. They rejoice when a new believer says, "Yes, I want to begin the pilgrimage of faith. Yes, I want to follow Jesus Christ." They find great joy and satisfaction in ministry fruit. They marvel as believers share their faith with those who do not know the good news. They celebrate as the church ministers to those in need, especially those who are economically poor or those who are spiritually impoverished.

And then fruitful leaders stand back and remember: We planted as carefully as we knew how. We watered and fertilized and pruned. We loved and nourished the vineyard God gave to us. And always we prayed.

After all we did, God gave the rich harvest. It was God who made it all grow. Fruitfulness is finally in God's hands.

SOMETIMES THE HARVEST IS LONG IN COMING

After we have done all we can, we would do well to recall the reminder of Marian Wright Edelman that "many fruits of your labor will not become manifest for many, many years."[4] Fruitful leadership leaves a legacy not just in the achievements we see but in outcomes that come to fruition over a very long time. Most of us have had the experience of learning of our influence upon another person about which we were unaware at the time it happened. So it is with congregations. The impact of efforts today can only be seen dimly no matter how carefully we monitor results. We will never know what a congregation is doing in the lives of countless people who will, as a result, bear much fruit of their own. Even in what seem to be failures, we may discover years later that the idea planted long before and rejected has now taken root and is bearing good fruit.

GOD'S FRUITFULNESS IS UNPREDICTABLE

Orchard workers know that after all the time, energy, and effort they put forth, they do not control the shape of the harvest. Similarly, in our congregations we are cultivating fruitfulness, not success. Good planning and hard work may bring success, but fruitfulness is possible only through the power of God.

We will have goals, but our primary mission is to do God's will. We do our very best to see that all we do is mission shaped. And sometimes the fruit we anticipate is not the harvest that God grants. But if we are faithful in seeking to know and pursue God's vision to the best of our ability, God is able to take our imperfect efforts and create out of them fruit both different and beyond what we anticipated. We learn to stop thinking we control the fruit that God will produce. God takes our faithfulness in fruitfulness and uses it in God's own way and time.

This is the reason that efforts sometimes appear as failures. The original outcome was not reached, but God has worked to accomplish a different—and often greater—outcome. Indeed, it is true that "God's foolishness is wiser than human wisdom" (1 Corinthians 1:25).

Lovett had a personal experience that brought this lesson home to him. After doing well in elementary school, his son Lawrence began to get increasingly lower grades at the beginning of middle school.

Lawrence is the youngest of our four children. I had always felt good about how close I was to each child, but there seemed to be an emotional distance between Lawrence and me. I came to see later that some things I had benefited from in spending time with the first three children were not in play for Lawrence. When the first three were young, I was a pastor. Much of our family life centered around the local church and also the denominational activities that we always did as a family.

When Lawrence was young, I had become a seminary administrator. Commuting to a job that had little connection to the family had results I only later realized. I had failed to make sufficient changes in my routines to bond closely with Lawrence. The gap between us was real. All members of the family were aware of it, and none of us knew what to do about it.

As Lawrence's grades kept going down, my wife, Emily, and I did all the normal things that parents do to encourage better schoolwork. We met with teachers and monitored homework. Finally, we had a session with teachers, counselors, and Lawrence, and we developed a game plan for improvement.

My main assignment was to work with Lawrence every school night on social studies. When I was out of town, we did it by telephone. I used every tutoring technique I knew. At the end of each evening, I questioned him on the unit, and he always knew the answers. I was feeling good about the whole endeavor.

When the report card came as summer began, his social studies grade had changed: after weeks of my tutoring, his grade had gone down! I was devastated.

Much happened that summer that seemed to help him gain confidence, though we will probably never know what made the difference. But the next year his grades were back up and stayed that way through high school and college.

He was fine, but I was not. I could not understand how my work with him had failed so badly. And then one day I realized that the great emotional gap that had always been between us was gone. Lawrence realized it also, as did the rest of the family, though there was no need to talk about it. We just celebrated what had happened. Lawrence and I are as close today as any father and son, and it is hard to imagine that it was ever different.

As so many others have experienced in their families and in their congregations, God took what looked like a failure and wrestled out of it a blessing.

Maintaining Hope When You're Not Winning

"The final resting place of the religious spirit," said Howard Thurman, "is that the basis of hope is never ultimately to be found in the course of events."[5] If success is the goal, it is very hard to maintain hope when things consistently seem to go wrong. Fruitful leadership is far more than merely the human endeavor of setting goals and accomplishing them. While there are goals and the monitoring of those goals, the final worth of the pastor and congregation is not synonymous with those outcomes. Therefore, the hope required to keep going comes not through accomplishing every endeavor but through knowing that God is with us and will never leave us. And our hope is sure because it comes not from what God may do in the future but from what God has already done. God has brought us this far and will not leave us orphaned.

Paul said it this way: "We are often troubled, but not crushed; sometimes in doubt, but never in despair; there are many enemies, but we are never without a friend; and though badly hurt at times, we are not destroyed" (2 Corinthians 4:8-9 GNT).

After the plowing,
> after the planting, and
>> after the long days of tending...
>>> *then*
>>>> the harvest comes.

Let us not be weary in well doing: for in due season we
shall reap, if we faint not. (Galatians 6:9 KJV)

Today, I make my Sacrament of Thanksgiving....
I pass before me the mainsprings of my heritage:
The fruits of the labors of countless generations who lived before me, without whom my own life would have no meaning;
The seers who saw visions and dreamed dreams;
The prophets who sensed a truth greater than the mind could grasp, and whose words could only find fulfillment in the years which they would never see;...
The saviors whose blood was shed with a recklessness that only a dream could inspire and God could command.
For all this I make an act of Thanksgiving this day.[6]

Howard Thurman

AREN'T YOU AMAZED BY WHAT GOD CAN DO?

TOM BERLIN

The frenetic pace of some workdays can elevate the decision to take a phone call at 4:55 p.m. to the level of a moral dilemma. It had been one of those days for me—full of meetings, phone calls, and individual appointments. It had also been a particularly exciting day, and I was eager to get home and share it with my family. Looking at the number listed on my phone by caller ID, I knew this was a call from Walt, the chair of our church council. Walt and I had been working together in a variety of capacities for the entire ten years I had served as pastor at Floris United Methodist Church. Recalling all the time we had spent together as well as his ample gift for encouragement, I picked up the phone.

"Tell me what you have been doing today," Walt said. "What good things are happening in our church?"

Many things ran through my mind.

- Leaders of our building committee met with the architect to discuss the plans for phase two of the new facility. After thirteen years in its second facility, Floris moved to a new site and its third facility to accommodate the growth of the congregation. Phase two, a sanctuary, would be our greatest challenge yet.

- The mission team that was working with the United Methodist Church in Sierra Leone, Africa, had established a timeline for the opening of Mercy Hospital, a medical center that would serve the economically poor in Bo, Sierra Leone.
- Staff members had stopped in to discuss their ministry areas and their hopes to move them to a new level of fruitfulness.
- Kevin Bacon, the actor, had called to interview me and Ginny, a church member who had led us to become one of the top six finalists in Bacon's SixDegrees.org challenge. Bacon had challenged nonprofit organizations to extend their fund-raising by creating a contest, with the top six nonprofits that had the largest number of donors over $10 receiving a $10,000 grant from Kevin Bacon. Ginny is one of the key leaders in the Child Rescue Centre, the residential home for war-affected orphans in Sierra Leone that is supported by our church and, at that time, seven other partner congregations.

As I shared some of these highlights, I became more and more aware of what a blessed day it had been.

Walt listened patiently and then replied, "Tom, if I had told you ten years ago that I would call you today to discuss the second phase of a facility where we had to relocate because of the growth of the church, the exciting ministry plans the church staff are implementing, and your conversation with a Hollywood actor about a children's home and hospital our church helped found in one of the poorest countries in the world, you would have told me that I was crazy. Aren't you amazed by what God can do?"

He was exactly right. After I finished my conversation with Walt, I sat in my office and thought about his question. I thought back over the past ten years of ministry at Floris and the ten years prior to that in other congregations. I was amazed at how far God had exceeded my expectations regarding the vitality and fruitfulness of ministry through these congregations.

Such moments of clarity produce a deep humility when a pastor fully understands the sense of wonder and confidence in God found in the apostle Paul's prayer for the church in Ephesus: "Now to him who by the power at work within us is able to accomplish abundantly far more than all we can ask or imagine, to him be glory in the church and in Christ Jesus to all generations, for ever and ever. Amen" (Ephesians 3:20-21).

As we wrote this book about fruitful leadership in the church, we did so with a great deal of humility. The denomination we serve has been shrinking since 1966. The story told in this book about Floris Church is not a dramatic story of overnight success. The congregation is more than 120 years old! Nor is it an especially large church by the standards of today's large teaching churches. But we believe there are lessons to be learned from a church with many flaws and imperfections that has been around a long time but has been able to show consistent and healthy growth for a number of years. And at the same time, it has pursued a new vision for others far beyond anything that could have been imagined a few years ago.

We believe that it is God's will for churches to be healthy and fruitful in their ministry. We believe that it is possible for congregations to experience vitality, but that such vitality will require a certain type of leadership. Fruitful congregations require fruitful leadership. Fruitful leadership is possible for pastors and lay leaders in churches today. This book is an attempt to describe that leadership and the key issues that will enable the growth of the church.

We close with these words of hope from the poetry of Marge Piercy. She encourages us to persevere in the work that is before us, knowing that it will have to go on for a long time. But then, she assures us:

> ...every gardener knows that after the digging, after the planting, after the long season of tending and growth, the harvest comes.[1]

NOTES

INTRODUCTION

1. The research was conducted between 2006 and 2009 for the development of the Lewis Pastoral Leadership Inventory™ (LPLI), a 360-degree pastoral leadership assessment instrument now available at www.lpli.org. The research involved fifteen hundred clergy in the United States from different denominations, regions, genders, ages, church sizes, and racial and ethnic groups.

2. Sarah B. Drummond, *Holy Clarity: The Practice of Planning and Evaluation* (Herndon, Va.: Alban, 2009), 59.

3. Church leaders may be surprised to find that many in the business world shy away from evaluation because they believe that their intangibles cannot be measured. A technical book addressing how to measure virtually anything is by Douglas W. Hubbard, *How to Measure Anything: Finding the Value of Intangibles in Business* (New York: John Wiley & Sons, 2007).

4. "We can begin to see . . . why evaluation literature has begun to describe evaluation as an act of leadership." Drummond then gives examples of ways in which "evaluation is an act of leadership, not just reporting" (*Holy Clarity*, 53).

1. A BIBLICAL MANDATE FOR FRUITFULNESS

1. Robert Schnase, "Pruning for Greater Fruitfulness," *United Methodist Reporter*, November 5, 2009.

2. AN INVITATION TO LABOR FOR GOD'S HARVEST

1. "A Ten Year Old Mission Statement," from Andy Bryan's blog, *Enter the Rainbow*, http://entertherainbow.blogspot.com/, January 25, 2010.

2. Sue Mallory, "You Get What You Measure," *Rev!* magazine, September-October 2006, 111.

3. Gil Rendle and Susan Beaumont, *When Moses Meets Aaron: Staffing and Supervision in Large Congregations* (Herndon, Va.: Alban, 2007), 41.

4. Robert Schnase, *Five Practices of Fruitful Congregations* (Nashville: Abingdon Press, 2007), 135–36.

5. David McAllister-Wilson, "Fruitful Leadership for a Mission-Shaped Church," *Leading Ideas* (Lewis Center for Church Leadership), November 9, 2005.

6. "The World Is Our Vineyard," *Circuit Rider*, November-December-January 2007–2008, 26.

7. Hans Conzelmann, *First Corinthians* (Philadelphia: Fortress Press, 1975), 83.

8. John Wesley, "Minutes of Several Conversations" (also known as the "Large Minutes"), Question 50, *The Works of the Rev. John Wesley, A.M.*, ed. Thomas Jackson, 3rd ed. (London: John Mason, 1831), 8:324–35.

3. THE TWO MOST POWERFUL WORDS FOR FRUITFUL LEADERSHIP

1. Dave Ulrich, Jack Zenger, and Norm Smallwood, *Results-Based Leadership* (Boston: Harvard Business School Press, 1999), 179.

4. FROM FRUITFUL MANAGEMENT TO FRUITFUL LEADERSHIP

1. Lovett H. Weems Jr., *Take the Next Step: Leading Lasting Change in the Church* (Nashville: Abingdon Press, 2003).

2. In addition to Lovett's book *Take the Next Step*, other books that some churches may consider for use in their planning include Carl S. Dudley and Nancy T. Ammerman, *Congregations in Transition: A Guide for Analyzing, Assessing, and Adapting in Changing Communities* (San Francisco: Jossey-Bass, 2002); Gil Rendle and Alice Mann, *Holy Conversations: Strategic Planning as a Spiritual Practice for Congregations* (Herndon, Va.: Alban, 2003); Daniel P. Smith and Mary K. Sellon, *Pathway to Renewal: Practical Steps for Congregations* (Herndon, Va.: Alban, 2008); Will Mancini, *Church Unique: How Missional Leaders Cast Vision, Capture Culture, and Create Movement* (San Francisco: Jossey-Bass, 2008); and Bud Wrenn, *Innovative Planning: Your Church in 4-D* (St. Louis: Chalice Press, 2008).

5. FRUITFUL LEADERSHIP IN ESTABLISHED CONGREGATIONS

1. Robert K. Martin, "Church Leadership Holds Much in Common with Gardening," *Missouri Conference Review*, May 5, 2006.

2. Steven B. Sample, *The Contrarian's Guide to Leadership* (San Francisco: Jossey-Bass, 2003), 145. Learning and telling a congregation's story, along with tying that story to the church's historic story and the congregation's current vision, is a major role for fruitful pastoral leaders. The Alban Institute has published the Narrative Leadership Collection of three books: *Finding Our Story: Narrative Leadership and Congregational Change*, *Teaching Our Story: Narrative Leadership and Pastoral Formation*, and *Living Our Story: Narrative Leadership and Congregational Culture*, all edited by Larry A. Golemon (Herndon, Va.: Alban, 2010). One particularly insightful chapter is by N. Graham Standish, "Pastor as Narrative Leader," in *Living Our Story*, 63–88.

7. GIVING LIFE TO THE VISION

1. Adam Hamilton, pastor of the United Methodist Church of the Resurrection in Leawood, Kansas, writes weekly e-mails that illustrate well these criteria. You may view them at the church's website, www.cor.org.
2. Michael Slaughter, *Money Matters: Financial Freedom for All God's Churches* (Nashville: Abingdon Press, 2006), 48–51. Helpful examples are also found in the appendix.

8. SUSTAINING FRUITFUL LEADERSHIP

1. "The World Is Our Vineyard," *Circuit Rider*, November-December-January 2007–2008, 25.
2. Paul Brand and Philip Yancey, *Pain: The Gift Nobody Wants* (New York: HarperCollins, 1993), 92–102.
3. Jim Loehr and Tony Schwartz, *The Power of Full Engagement* (New York: Free Press, 2003), 32.

9. PLANTING, WATERING, AND PRAYING FOR GROWTH

1. Robert Schnase, *Five Practices of Fruitful Congregations* (Nashville: Abingdon Press, 2007), 134.
2. Tim Stevens and Tony Morgan, *Simply Strategic Growth* (Loveland, Colo.: Group Publishing, 2005), 110.
3. Robin Gill, *A Vision for Growth* (London: SPCK, 1994), 13–14.

4. Marian Wright Edelman, *The Measure of Our Success* (Boston: Beacon Press, 1992), 59.

5. Howard Thurman, "Habakkuk," in *The Interpreter's Bible*, vol. 6 (Nashville: Abingdon Press, 1956), 1002.

6. Howard Thurman, *Meditations of the Heart* (1953; repr., Richmond, Ind.: Friends United Press, 1976), 148–49.

EPILOGUE

1. Marge Piercy, "The Seven of Pentacles," in *In Praise of Fertile Land*, edited by Claudia Mauro (Seattle: Whit Press, 2006).

CPSIA information can be obtained at www.ICGtesting.com
Printed in the USA
BVOW04s2017180514

353785BV00014B/156/P